Remembering the Crusades in Medieval Texts and Songs

Special Issue of
*The Journal of Religious History,
Literature and Culture*
2019

Edited by
ANDREW D. BUCK and THOMAS W. SMITH

Volume 5 November 2019 Number 2
UNIVERSITY OF WALES PRESS
https://doi.org/10.16922/jrhlc.5.2

Editors
Professor William Gibson, Oxford Brookes University
Dr John Morgan-Guy, University of Wales Trinity Saint David

Assistant Editor
Dr Thomas W. Smith, Rugby School

Reviews Editor
Dr Nicky Tsougarakis, Edge Hill University

Editorial Advisory Board
Professor David Bebbington, Stirling University
Professor Stewart J. Brown, University of Edinburgh
Dr James J. Caudle, Yale University
Dr Robert G. Ingram, Ohio University, USA
Professor Geraint Jenkins, Aberystwyth University
Dr David Ceri Jones, Aberystwyth University
Professor J. Gwynfor Jones, Cardiff University
Dr Paul Kerry, Brigham Young University, USA
Dr Frances Knight, University of Nottingham
Dr Robert Pope, University of Wales Trinity Saint David
Professor Huw Pryce, Bangor University
Professor Kenneth E. Roxburgh, Samford University, USA
Dr Eryn M. White, Aberystwyth University
Rt Revd and Rt Hon. Lord Williams of Oystermouth,
Magdalene College, Cambridge
Professor Jonathan Wooding, University of Sydney, Australia

Editorial Contacts
wgibson@brookes.ac.uk
j.morgan-guy@uwtsd.ac.uk
TWS@rugbyschool.net
tsougarn@edgehill.ac.uk

Publishers and book reviewers with enquiries regarding reviews should contact the journal's reviews editor.

In memory of Bernard Hamilton

CONTENTS

The Contributors — vii
Editorial — ix
Abbreviations — xi

'Weighed by such a great calamity, they were cleansed for their sins': Remembering the Siege and Capture of Antioch
Andrew D. Buck — 1

Framing the Narrative of the First Crusade: The Letter Given at Laodicea in September 1099
Thomas W. Smith — 17

Fear, Fortitude and Masculinity in William of Malmesbury's Retelling of the First Crusade and the Establishment of the Latin East
Stephen J. Spencer — 35

Refocusing the First Crusade: Authorial Self-Fashioning and the Miraculous in William of Tyre's *Historia Ierosolymitana*
Beth C. Spacey — 51

Remembering Jerusalem: Lamenting the Holy City in Occitan Lyric, c. 1187–c. 1300
Lauren Mulholland — 67

'Li bons dus de Buillon': Genre Conventions and the Depiction of Godfrey of Bouillon in the *Chanson d'Antioche* and the *Chanson de Jérusalem*
Simon John — 83

The *Gran conquista de Ultramar*, its Precursors, and the Lords of Saint-Pol
Simon Thomas Parsons — 101

Index — 117

THE CONTRIBUTORS

Andrew D. Buck is Government of Ireland Postdoctoral Research Fellow, University College Dublin and a fellow of the Royal Historical Society. He is the author of *The Principality of Antioch and its Frontiers in the Twelfth Century* (The Boydell Press, 2017) as well as several articles on the history of the principality of Antioch and the broader history of the Latin East. His current project examines the *Chronicon* of Archbishop William of Tyre and the writing of history in *Outremer*.

Simon John is Senior Lecturer in Medieval History at Swansea University. His research interests include the socio-cultural impact of the crusades in Latin Christendom, remembrances of the First Crusade in the Middle Ages, and political thought on medieval kingship. He is the author of *Godfrey of Bouillon: Duke of Lower Lotharingia, Ruler of Latin Jerusalem, c. 1060–1100* (Routledge, 2018), and has published articles in the *English Historical Review*, the *Journal of Medieval History* and the *Journal of Ecclesiastical History*.

Lauren Mulholland completed her PhD at the School of History, Queen Mary University of London, in 2019. Her thesis examines representations of the Holy Land in Occitan lyric and literature. Her main research interests are in medieval devotional culture and vernacular literature, particularly in Occitan and Old French.

Simon Thomas Parsons is a Teaching Fellow in Medieval History at King's College London. He has written several articles and book chapters on Anglo-Norman crusade participation and the Latin and vernacular accounts of the First Crusade, has co-edited (with Linda Paterson) the collection of essays *Literature of the Crusades* (D. S. Brewer, 2018) and is preparing a monograph on the textual tradition of the early crusading movement.

Thomas W. Smith teaches history at Rugby School and is a fellow of the Royal Historical Society. He is the author of *Curia and Crusade: Pope Honorius III and the Recovery of the Holy Land, 1216–1227* (Brepols, 2017), which was Highly Commended in the British Records

Association's Janette Harley Prize competition 2018. His second book, *The Letters of the First Crusade*, is forthcoming with the Boydell Press

Beth C. Spacey is a postdoctoral research fellow in the School of Historical and Philosophical Inquiry at the University of Queensland. She completed her doctorate at the University of Birmingham in 2017 and has published on miracles and masculinities in medieval Latin Christian crusades sources. Her book, *The Miraculous and the Writing of Crusade History*, is forthcoming with Boydell and Brewer.

Stephen J. Spencer is a *Past & Present* Postdoctoral Research Fellow at the Institute of Historical Research, University of London, where he is working on the memorialisation of the Third Crusade in western Europe before 1300. He has published several articles on the emotional rhetoric of crusading, and his first book, *Emotions in a Crusading Context, 1095–1291*, is forthcoming with Oxford University Press.

EDITORIAL

The cover image from Leeds, Brotherton Library, University of Leeds, BC MS 100/28, a late fifteenth-century manuscript roll containing an account of biblical and genealogical history from Adam and Eve until the time of King Louis XI of France, is a good avatar for this volume of essays on remembering crusades in medieval narratives, be they written or oral. The miniature depicts Godfrey of Bouillon's contingent on board a ship bound for the Holy Land on the First Crusade. Anyone with a rudimentary knowledge of the course of the First Crusade will know that none of the main armies travelled by sea (though some of the late Pisan and English contingents did indeed travel in this manner). It is not, therefore, an accurate guide to 'what really happened', but a valuable source for the medieval reception and remembrance of crusading deeds and histories. It is this approach to the memory of the crusades which informs the present publication. Exploring Latin texts, as well as Old French, Castilian and Occitan songs and lyrics, these essays contribute to new directions in crusade studies by offering a more nuanced understanding of the diverse ways in which medieval authors presented events, people, and places central to the crusading movement. From exploring how the transmission of stories related to suffering, heroism, the miraculous and ideals of masculinity helped to shape ideas of crusading, to the importance of Jerusalem in the lyric cultures of southern France, and how the narrative arc of the First Crusade developed from the earliest written and oral responses to the venture, this volume thus aims to provide new perspectives on well-known topics while simultaneously bringing new ones to light. Our thanks go to Bill Gibson and John Morgan-Guy for their fulsome support of this volume, and to Henry Maas for his careful work as copy-editor. Finally, it was with great sadness that we learned of the death of Bernard Hamilton while this volume was in production. An outstanding historian of the crusades, Bernard did so much to encourage the study of the topic, especially among emerging scholars. It was our great pleasure to offer this volume as a small token of gratitude for everything he had done for us; now, with heavy hearts, we dedicate it to the memory of a brilliant scholar and a true gentleman.

Andrew D. Buck
Thomas William Smith

ABBREVIATIONS

AA	Albert of Aachen, *Historia Hierosolimitana*, ed. and trans. S. B. Edgington, Oxford Medieval Texts (Oxford, 2007)
BB	Baldric of Bourgueil, *Historia Ierosolimitana*, ed. S. Biddlecombe (Woodbridge, 2014)
ChAnt	*La Chanson d'Antioche*, ed. S. Duparc-Quioc, 2 vols, Documents relatifs à l'histoire des croisades publiés par l'Académie des Inscriptions et Belles Lettres, 11 (Paris, 1977–8)
Chétifs	*La Chanson des Chétifs*, ed. G. M. Myers, *OFCC*, vol. 5
ChJér	*La Chanson de Jérusalem*, ed. N. R. Thorp, *OFCC*, vol. 6
FC	Fulcher of Chartres, *Historia Hierosolymitana*, ed. H. Hagenmeyer (Heidelberg, 1913)
GF	*Gesta Francorum et aliorum Hierosolimitanorum*, ed. and trans. R. Hill, Oxford Medieval Texts (Oxford, 1962)
GN	Guibert of Nogent, *Dei gesta per Francos*, ed. R. B. C. Huygens, Corpus Christianorum, Continuatio Mediaeualis, 127A (Turnhout, 1996)
GP	Gilo of Paris, *Historia vie Hierosolimitane*, ed. and trans. C. W. Grocock and E. J. Siberry, Oxford Medieval Texts (Oxford, 1997)
HH	Henry of Huntingdon, *Historia Anglorum: The History of the English People*, ed. and trans. D. F. Greenway, Oxford Medieval Texts (Oxford, 1996)
Kb	*Epistulae et chartae ad historiam primi belli sacri spectantes quae supersunt aevo aequales et genuinae / Die Kreuzzugsbriefe aus den Jahren 1088–1100: Eine Quellensammlung zur Geschichte des ersten Kreuzzuges*, ed. H. Hagenmeyer (Innsbruck, 1901)
MGH	Monumenta Germaniae Historica
OFCC	*The Old French Crusade Cycle*, ed. J. A. Nelson and E. J. Mickel, 10 vols in 11 (Tuscaloosa, AL, 1977–2003)
OV	Orderic Vitalis, *The Ecclesiastical History of Orderic Vitalis*, ed. and trans. M. Chibnall, 6 vols, Oxford Medieval Texts (Oxford, 1969–80)
PT	Peter Tudebode, *Historia de Hierosolymitano itinere*, ed. J. H. Hill and L. L. Hill (Paris, 1977)

RA	Raymond of Aguilers, *Le 'Liber' de Raymond d'Aguilers*, ed. J. H. Hill and L. L. Hill, Documents relatifs à l'histoire des croisades, 9 (Paris, 1969)
RC	Ralph of Caen, 'Gesta Tancredi in Expeditione Hierosolymitana', in *Recueil des Historiens des Croisades: Documents Occidentaux*, ed. Académie des Inscriptions et Belles-Lettres, 5 vols (Paris, 1844–95), vol. 3, pp. 599–716
RM	Robert the Monk, *Historia Iherosolimitana*, ed. D. Kempf and M. G. Bull (Woodbridge, 2013)
WM	William of Malmesbury, *Gesta regum Anglorum*, ed. and trans. R. A. B. Mynors, R. M. Thomson, and M. Winterbottom, 2 vols, Oxford Medieval Texts (Oxford, 1998–9)
WT	William of Tyre, *Chronicon*, ed. R. B. C. Huygens, Corpus Christianorum, Continuatio Mediaevalis, 63/63A (Turnhout, 1986)

'WEIGHED BY SUCH A GREAT CALAMITY, THEY WERE CLEANSED FOR THEIR SINS': REMEMBERING THE SIEGE AND CAPTURE OF ANTIOCH

Andrew D. Buck

On 28 June 1098, the forces of the First Crusade, outnumbered and desperate, achieved an astounding victory over the forces of Kerbogha, *atabeg* of Mosul, outside the north Syrian city of Antioch.[1] With this, Muslim resistance to the city's capture crumbled, and, perhaps more importantly, after a gruelling eight-month siege the expedition had received confirmation, so many contemporary commentators believed, of God's divine favour. The events of October 1097–June 1098 certainly left a lasting impression: Latin chroniclers expended much ink on their telling and retelling, with the story of Antioch's capture often emerging as the longest distinct stage of the crusade in contemporary narratives.[2] Through these processes, the memory of the siege and capture of Antioch during the First Crusade was crafted as one of the venture's main proving grounds: a moment in which God tested the faith and dedication of his soldiers, allowing them to demonstrate their worthiness to recover Jerusalem and the Holy Sepulchre. Accordingly, the sources are replete with descriptions of intense suffering and acts of devotional bravery, as well as cowardice and the transgression of social bonds and structures – a comparative series of themes undoubtedly used by ecclesiastical authors to outline the idealised characteristics of a holy warrior. In short, the events at Antioch became a central node in the processes of remembering and defining the First Crusade.

Nevertheless, while modern scholarship on the interrelationship between crusading and memory has largely argued for a value-positive relationship – that is the transmission of the crusading past served to promote future activities – this piece tests this assumption by reconsidering the ways in which authors constructed and transmitted the memory of the siege and battle of Antioch, and how these events emerged as a core didactic moment in the ecclesiastical construction of the crusading ideal.[3] It argues, moreover, that an exploration of the underlying tensions and traumas reflected in the narratives can lay the groundwork for a more nuanced understanding of how memories of the crusade interacted with secular attitudes towards the physical act of crusading itself.

Before exploring the textual traditions surrounding Antioch, though, it is worth briefly outlining the general narrative arc of the siege. Arriving in October 1097, the crusaders' supplies quickly ran out, while conditions in the camp deteriorated during the harsh winter. Meanwhile, although the crusaders withstood the continual harassment of Antioch's garrison, and successfully faced off Muslim armies from Damascus (December 1097) and Aleppo (February 1098), major foraging expeditions failed to alleviate shortages. Increased levels of suffering led to the dispersal of Latin forces and even desertion. It was only in spring 1098 that the situation changed, as the failure of Muslim relief armies and the construction of makeshift crusader fortresses weakened the garrison's resolve. The arrival of Latin ships at the nearby port of St Symeon also increased food supplies. However, towards June 1098, news spread of the major Muslim army led by Kerbogha, causing one leader, Stephen of Blois, to depart, and another, Bohemond of Taranto, to hatch a plan to engineer the city's fall by colluding with a tower guard called Firuz. Though Antioch was subsequently captured on 3 June 1098, the citadel held out, meaning Kerbogha's arrival the next day left the crusaders trapped between two forces. As a result, they endured three weeks of extreme suffering, with intense Muslim attacks, famine and disease causing many to secretly flee the city and desert the venture. Morale was only maintained by strong leadership and the apparent finding of a relic of the Holy Lance. In response to this discovery, or perhaps simply the desperate reality of their situation, the crusaders faced Kerbogha in open battle on 28 June, achieving an unlikely victory. Antioch was secured, and the crusaders could embark on several months of recuperation before continuing their journey.[4]

The Penitent and Suffering Warrior

Suffering is a dominant theme of contemporary narratives of the siege of Antioch; indeed, all accounts present suffering as an ever-present and crucial spectre, one that played an important role in defining the ideal crusader.

This can be seen throughout the participant narratives. The earliest of these is probably the *Gesta Francorum*, whose anonymous author spent the months at Antioch in Bohemond of Taranto's contingent.[5] The author described the crusaders's 'immense misfortune and misery', noting that 'we suffered these, and many anxieties and extremities which I am unable to name, for the name of Christ and to deliver the road to the Holy Sepulchre'.[6] It was, in short, a purifying ritual. Such suffering was also often coupled to a physical test; namely battle, in which courage and dedication in combat would meet with God's reward (victory and supplies). For example, when food shortages reached a critical state in early 1098, and the Byzantine guide, Tatikios, departed from the crusade, the Latins were faced with battle against Ridwan of Aleppo. Meeting the Muslim army head on 'in aid of God and the Holy Sepulchre', the crusaders' dedication and steadfast endurance ensured victory and supplies 'by God's will' (*Deo annuente*).[7] This narrative set-piece of suffering–battle–reward appeared throughout the *Gesta*'s account of the months at Antioch, with the ultimate symbol of God's favour being victory against Kerbogha with the aid of saintly warriors. Likewise, the *Gesta* repeatedly suggested that the crusaders were proving their worthiness to recover the Holy City by relating the struggle for Antioch to the journey (*iter*) to Jerusalem and the Holy Sepulchre.[8] As such, after victory, the crusade leaders met to decide 'how they might best lead and guide the people until they should complete the journey to the Holy Sepulchre, for which, thus far, they had already suffered many perils'.[9] The road to Jerusalem had thus been opened by the endurance and sacrifice experienced at Antioch.

Importantly, the other participant narratives include similar themes. Peter Tudebode's *Historia*, which exhibits close textual similarities to the *Gesta* bar some personal flourishes largely relating to the author's own experiences, mirrors the latter's content, while Raymond of Aguilers, who detailed events from within the camp of Count Raymond of Toulouse, noted that God inflicted suffering to scourge the crusaders and 'to rouse the minds of the shameful, adulterous and pillaging to repentance'.[10] He even suggested that by overcoming famine the crusaders shared such a bond as to be considered a confraternity (*confraternitatis*), and that through the discovery of the Holy Lance, 'His divine clemency [was manifested] . . . and that which had corrected the sons' lasciviousness

3

consoled the extreme sadness in this manner'.[11] The divine test was perhaps most clearly expressed by Fulcher of Chartres, who spent this period in Edessa with Baldwin of Boulogne, as he described the siege as 'the destitution of the Christians' – a test of faith and endurance, during which the Latins 'suffered the greatest hunger'.[12] Moreover, in suggesting that descent into avarice or pride caused such suffering, Fulcher drew on 1 Peter 1:6–7 – '[in] the trial of your faith (which is much more precious than gold, which is tried by fire) may be found . . . praise and glory and honour' – when noting that 'like gold thrice proved and purified seven times by fire, having been chosen by God . . . and weighed by such a great calamity, they were cleansed for their sins'.[13] In the participant narratives, therefore, the suffering at Antioch was cast as a divine test: those who passed it stayed, purged themselves of sin, and achieved victory.

There were some divergences, however, as Raymond and Fulcher both decried crusaders' desire for spoils or personal enjoyment, seeing these not as divine rewards, but symbolic of a greed antithetical to the ideal penitent warrior. Fulcher stated that God doubled the punishment during Kerbogha's siege because, once the crusaders had entered the city, many had 'immediately mingled with reckless women', while Raymond, after opining that many crusaders, even Bohemond, were concerned only with luxury, noted that

> while our men were counting and identifying the spoils, they desisted from besieging the upper castle, and, listening to the pagan dancing girls, had feasted sumptuously and arrogantly, remembering nothing of God, who had conferred such great kindness to them.[14]

Moreover, although neither Fulcher nor Raymond places the same emphasis on the road to Jerusalem as the *Gesta*, and Fulcher even went so far as also to omit the arrival of saintly knights in battle and to dismiss the veracity of the Holy Lance, all the participant narratives nevertheless incorporated textual discussions regarding the role of suffering and the extent to which earthly gain could, or indeed should, intersect with this new form of penitential warfare.[15]

Significantly, Antioch's role in the didactic formulation of the emerging crusading ethos, which emphasised the need to suffer in return for divine reward, only intensified with subsequent narrative retellings of the crusade. The most prominent of these were the Benedictine reworkings of the *Gesta*, written in the first decades of the twelfth century by

Robert the Monk, Baldric of Bourgeuil and Guibert of Nogent (who also utilised Fulcher's text).[16] Thus, both Baldric and Guibert stressed the purgative nature of the suffering, with the former suggesting that victories and spoils were gained through divine aid and that famine occurred because:

> God was mercifully reproving them in such a way that they would turn to Him with their heart, and if there was any lack of repentance lurking within them, they would be purged by the fire of compunction and tempered by the misfortune of want that had come upon them.[17]

Both Baldric and Guibert also tied this to the Holy Sepulchre, with the former noting that the crusaders 'suffered so many disasters in order to deserve the right to see the Sepulchre of their Lord God', and the latter detailing an attempt by Bohemond to raise flagging morale by telling the crusaders to 'keep in mind the purpose of this effort . . . redeeming Jerusalem for God and liberating His tomb'.[18] Guibert also described Antioch as a 'pious siege' (*piae obsidionis*) and an act 'holy suffering' (*sanctae passionis*), while illness caused by famine 'refreshed the vigour of the soul'.[19] Emphasising the devotional importance of endurance perhaps more than any author other than Fulcher, Guibert went further, suggesting that 'they were driven by hope for something better to rely on God alone, the only true support in such tribulation . . . [while] the more they watched their supplies diminish . . . the more they were taught to submit with appropriate humility to God'.[20] The crusaders were implored to 'offer your bravery for the suffering Christ'.[21] Overall, therefore, both continued the pattern of portraying events at Antioch as a crucial test, one in which extensive suffering had to be endured to open the path to Jerusalem.

Perhaps the most important text for tracing memorialisation processes, however, is that of Robert the Monk, as its wide manuscript tradition reveals its contemporary popularity – such that it is considered something of a medieval bestseller.[22] In this context, it is important that Robert built upon and extended the *Gesta* to provide a more theologically sound, and indeed more exciting, narrative. His account of the siege of Antioch thus begins with the statement that God wanted to regain the city 'so that the Lord might show mortal eyes that none are strong or powerful except through Him'.[23] Thereafter, Robert portrayed high levels of suffering as a means to earn divine reward through purgative endurance, noting how 'the harshness of the weather, the helpless misery of need, and the constriction of the enemy, weighed down upon them', but that hard-fought crusader victories, and their rewards, were 'great gifts from the supreme provider'.[24] Moreover, Robert imputed a speech to Bohemond in which he reminded doubting crusaders that God 'often tests his faithful, so that He may be made aware whether they may love Him'. 'Now', Robert continued, 'he tests you through troubles of hunger, and through the constant pressures of your enemies'.[25] He also stated that 'God wished that the city should be difficult to secure, so that having been gained it would be held dearly'.[26] Echoing both Raymond and Fulcher's comments regarding punishment for sexual incontinence, Robert included amongst a series of visions by a priest named Stephen of Valence a conversation with Christ, in which the latter remarked that 'all the tribulations and impediments they suffered, therefore, I allowed to happen, because they committed many sins with Christian and pagan women, which is greatly displeasing in my eyes'.[27] Through the familiar trope of carnal sin leading to further suffering, Robert perpetuated existing debates about the proper behaviour of a *miles Christi* and the consequences of not matching these expectations. He also furthered the narrative tradition linking Antioch to Jerusalem, relating how a Fatimid offer of peaceful entry into the Holy City made at Antioch was rejected because it 'will be ours not through human concession, but through the justice of divine decree', and detailed that the leaders accepted Bohemond's claim to Antioch because: 'none of us has left his land out of ambition for the city of Antioch; let him have it who God wishes to give it to. All of us have one intention, namely the liberation of the Holy Sepulchre'.[28] In short, like his Benedictine contemporaries, Robert presented Antioch as a crucial step towards recovering Jerusalem, a challenge that necessitated suffering and endurance.

Significantly, these trends are found in the works of three other early non-participant chroniclers of the crusade: Albert of Aachen, Gilo of Paris, and Ralph of Caen.[29] Indeed, even though Albert's *Historia*, unlike most other sources, sits outside the *Gesta* tradition, it nevertheless outlined the extent and penitential nature of the crusaders' suffering.[30] According to Albert, a 'very serious scarcity' (*gravissima penuria*) struck the 'people of the living God', resulting from their many sins.[31] It was only once the crusaders recognised this, and focused solely on prosecuting divine vengeance rather than their physical sustenance, that God granted them victory.[32] This was epitomised in a speech given by a Lombard priest, in which he exhorted his fellow crusaders, who were suffering famine, pestilence and death, 'not to believe you are undergoing this hardship for nothing, but listen and think of the reward which Lord Jesus will give back to all of those who will die for his love and favour on this journey'.[33] For Albert, like the other early chroniclers, suffering was a prerequisite to success, a trial that would bring divine reward once overcome.

Gilo of Paris, who drew heavily on Robert the Monk's text, similarly emphasised the penitential and divinely ordained nature of this attrition.[34] Thus, he detailed that 'those fighters for the faith regarded their excessive pains as merely bodily suffering, a small price to pay', and that 'their joy was not diminished by such punishments; nor did their good and constant minds falter due to these torments, however much their bodies suffered oppressive hardship'.[35] Gilo also recognised that victories were achieved 'by God's power' (*virtute Dei*), that Antioch had been granted to the crusaders because 'they had not faltered during such great burdens of suffering' ordered by God, and that those who died achieved martyrdom in return for their suffering.[36] In his *Gesta Tancredi*, Ralph of Caen likewise noted that 'everyone, the highest, those in the middle and the lowest, suffered badly', be it from hunger, the weather, or enemy attacks.[37] He even deployed the same biblical imagery of gold which 'having been tested by fire, is purged of impurities' used by Fulcher of Chartres, reasoning that, through these privations, God could reward the afflicted.[38]

What we find in the earliest written accounts of the crusade by both participants and non-participants, therefore, is an overarching narrative consistency in the depiction of events at Antioch as a holy trial, one in which suffering is represented as a divinely ordained opportunity for the crusaders to demonstrate their worthiness and as an important precursor to the attainment of spiritual and temporal rewards – particularly for the recovery of Jerusalem. This confirms the arguments made by modern historians who have suggested that the accounts produced by ecclesiastical authors sought to emphasise the crusade's Christo-mimetic characteristics and the value of suffering to participants' souls.[39] Despite this narrative consistency, however, a close reading of these texts can also reveal some important inconsistencies which might allow us to understand non-ecclesiastical attitudes towards crusader suffering.

Andrew D. Buck

Cowardice, Status and Social Bonds

As the suffering during the two sieges of Antioch grew, some fled from battle or chose to depart entirely, most prominently during the winter months of late 1097/early 1098 and during Kerbogha's siege. Yet, the sources detail these events in varied ways.

There are some continuities. For example, every source mentions at least one of the high-profile departures of Stephen of Blois and Hugh of Vermandois – the former being the most strongly criticised, with the author of the *Gesta Francorum* calling him 'wretched' (*infelix*) and Fulcher of Chartres stating that 'this act disgraced him'.[40] Moreover, nearly all of the authors discussed here presented the flight of crusaders during the armed struggle for Antioch as a deleterious act, with some arguing that it affected not only their reputations, but also those of their families in the West.[41] In particular, the *Gesta Francorum* described those who shied from the conflict as 'the most worthless of all Christians'; Raymond of Aguilers suggested they had given in to fear (*pavidi*) rather than trusting in God's mercy, and even accused deserters of spreading malicious lies about the venture; Robert the Monk insisted that they had perjured (*periurare*) themselves; Baldric of Bourgueil declared that they 'ran away quite disgracefully, to the shame of all their kin and descendants'; and Ralph of Caen criticised those of Norman heritage who – unlike his hero, Tancred of Hauteville – were unwilling to persevere and thus shamed (*pudendar*) the entire *gens* through their cowardly behaviour.[42] Likewise, although Gilo of Paris generally refrained from mentioning cowardice, his account of the events at Antioch ends with an invective dismissal of participants who failed to stay the course: 'I blot out from my book – from any book whatsoever – those who were not ashamed to carry themselves away from the fighting; this pitiable company, as if called back to vomit, [and] allied to the world, preferred exile to their homeland.'[43]

However, while several sources transmitted other common names of deserters, such as William the Carpenter, the Grandmesnil brothers and Guy the Red, constable of France, uniformity is lacking.[44] Indeed, some chroniclers, like Fulcher of Chartres, Robert the Monk, Guibert of Nogent and Gilo of Paris, were willing to report and criticise desertion but overtly chose not to name certain – sometimes all – of the aforementioned crusaders. The most common reason for this, alluded to above, is that it would cast shame on their families, with Guibert in particular stating that he would have provided the exact details of two Normans who fled from Antioch 'were I not bound by close friendship with their kin to limit my remarks, [and] thus to spare them from being entirely subdued by shame'.[45] In a similar vein, the Anglo-Norman historian, Orderic Vitalis, who incorporated an abridged version of Baldric of Bourgueil's *Historia* into his broader chronicle, edited his base text in such a way that the Grandmesnil brothers (whose family had close links to Orderic's monastery of St Evroult) did not appear to be exceptional cases, which had the effect of downplaying the shame attributed to the wider family and the monastic community.[46] There were also efforts to rehabilitate the reputations of Stephen of Blois and Hugh of Vermandois, or at least to lessen the level of criticism, either by not mentioning their departures or by noting their returns to the East and subsequent deaths during the 1101 Crusade. Baldric of Bourgueil even argued that God had engineered Stephen's departure so that Alexios would not come to Antioch and seize the city for himself.[47]

Importantly, these inconsistencies tap into broader tensions within the narratives. Rather than simple opprobrium, several authors adopted a rather more sympathetic tone towards those who fled the siege, with some coming close to suggesting that flight in the face of extreme famine – albeit not in the face of battle – was an understandable, if regrettable, reaction. Robert the Monk suggested that 'nor is it strange if human frailty should murmur under the weight of such great suffering', while in detailing the flight of William the Carpenter, he expressed hope that this was not due to fear of battle, but rather 'because he had never experienced the unjust suffering of such greater hunger'.[48] Most prominently, though, the sources acknowledge that the level of suffering experienced was unprecedented and that it also damaged and transgressed social bonds, structures and rituals. For the *Gesta Francorum*, the suffering was too great to describe, particularly during Kerbogha's siege, while nearly all authors mention the deaths of horses, the reduction of knights to the status of foot-soldier, the rusting or sale of weapons (particularly swords), and how extreme poverty acted as a social leveller as it affected the lower classes and elites alike. Fulcher of Chartres therefore lamented that 'our knights had been forced to become foot-soldiers; weak, helpless'; Raymond of Aguilers laid especial emphasis on the significance of the loss of horses; Gilo of Paris decried how poverty led to the breaking of social and familial bonds, with a knight rejecting his squire, a father his son, and a brother his brother; while Ralph of Caen suggested that the winter months were 'much harsher for the nobles, in as much as the peasant is tougher than the knight, as a toiler is to one accustomed to luxury', and that the sons of dukes, counts and kings 'were enclosed in a manner that had not happened before . . . nor since'.[49] 'Only those who have never heard anything like it', remarked Albert of Aachen, 'marvel at these miseries and impoverishments of the noble leaders'.[50] Finally, while all authors denote the suffering and death of the crusader forces, there are few, if any, mentions of the burial practices of the army while at Antioch; Peter Tudebode's mention of his brother's internment and Ralph of Caen's allusion to the grave of Conon of Brittany near the Iron Bridge are rare exceptions.[51]

Consequently, while it is likely that medieval commentators on the crusade utilised suffering and the breaking or transgressing of social bonds as a didactic tool to demonstrate that all were equal in the eyes of God, and that such markers of earthly status must be eschewed during acts of penitence, that they felt it necessary to comment (or remain conspicuously silent) on these, and in so doing created tensions within their narratives, could indicate that they were responding to concerns voiced outside the Church. Indeed, as Katherine Allen Smith has demonstrated, early crusading texts and attitudes were not simply a conversation between ecclesiastics. Rather, they reveal an ongoing dialogue between the secular and spiritual spheres.[52] It is certainly true that most authors made use of oral testimony in constructing their texts.[53] As such, while it would be wrong to suggest that Latin texts were written *for* secular audiences – even if the parallels found between the works of Robert the Monk and Albert of Aachen and the Old French prose account of the siege and battle of Antioch, the *Chanson d'Antioche*, reveal that they were far from ignorant of their content – it is nevertheless likely that, if read against the grain, these narratives can offer a window, if an imperfect one, onto the negative memories that circulated in elite circles.[54]

It is significant, therefore, that the tensions which emerge each tapped into an important aspect of elite culture in medieval Europe. Regarding the implications of desertion, this is perhaps obvious, for several authors recognised that such cowardly behaviour would have a lasting impact on reputations and social standing, just as success could bring long-term celebrity. Given the spiritual nature of the venture, it might also damage their immortal soul.[55] However, the loss of horses and weapons was also significant, because this not only undermined an individual's status as a knight (and perhaps as a noble), but, when combined with poverty and the breaking of social and familial bonds, could also impinge upon important dynastic identities and structures.[56] Likewise, the lack of references to burials transgressed a key means by which families might remember their dead through tomb visits, processions, and liturgy.[57] Nicholas Paul has argued that fears over the remains of the fallen might have been assuaged by belief that crusading led to martyrdom (although this is unlikely to have been widespread) or the use of prayers for the dead.[58] However, whereas the capture of Jerusalem in July 1099 was liturgically immortalised, giving Western families the chance to performatively remember their dead kin even if they did not have access to their remains, no such tradition grew up around the taking of Antioch.[59] Concerns over how the dead at Antioch should be properly remembered might thus have been keenly felt amongst aristocratic families. That there is an underlying sense that the authors felt the need to rationalise, explain or deflect attention away from issues of cowardice, desertion and the transgressing of social bonds, markers and rituals, could therefore indicate that, although ecclesiastics were convinced of the Christo-mimetic value of crusading, those charged with undertaking the venture, along with their families in the West, may have been less convinced.

Conclusion: Trauma and Memory

In a recent article, Megan Cassidy-Welch has argued for the potential value of exploring the crusading past through the prism of trauma theory, noting that:

> the relationship between individual experience and collective identifications that lay at the heart of medieval crusading culture can be illuminated by attention to contemporaneous theories of cognition, experience, memory and suffering, all of which are elements of trauma theory.[60]

Moreover, as Geoffrey Cubitt has outlined in *History and Memory*, narratives which coalesce around specific moments of trauma, particularly those in which the suffering experienced threatens both personal memory and the social structures which facilitate group remembrance, can lead to a 'selective reworking of remembered detail'. In such instances, those describing the trauma look to craft their own versions of events, and thus achieve some sense of personal ownership over the past. Through this, however, narrative consistency is often lost, making way instead for a 'crisis in the organisation of ... remembering'.[61] Consequently, while Cassidy-Welch has traced the effects of traumatic memory in moments of crusading failure, namely the loss of the True Cross at the Battle of Hattin in 1187, the evidence examined here suggests that similar insights might be gleaned from those episodes which, taken as a whole, could be considered successes for the crusading movement, like the siege and battle of Antioch.

Therefore, although the emphasis on the rewards for suffering came to define the nascent ethos behind this new form of penitential warfare, placing Antioch as a central node in the textual legitimising processes of crusading and a useful ecclesiastical didactic tool for better emphasising the Christo-mimetic ideal, the likelihood is that stories about those who failed to endure such hardships, saw their social status or bonds diminish, or failed to receive a proper burial, also transgressed core aspects of the emerging concepts of knighthood, nobility and familial honour, which were all important means by which future crusades might be promoted. As such, while Albert of Aachen wrote that 'those wonderful and unbelievable things which were done during the siege of Antioch cannot, I think, be recorded by any pen, any memory', because 'so many and such various things are reported to have happened there', it is clear that medieval commentators *did* expend a great deal of effort in trying to explain and rationalise these events, more so even than the capture of Jerusalem.[62] Whereas some scholars have seen in this efforts, exposed most prominently in the *Gesta Francorum*, to present Antioch as the First Crusade's climax, the aforementioned narrative inconsistencies perhaps instead reveal something of the underlying traumas the siege created within those elite circles which would have been considered the most receptive to the crusading message and the attempts made to respond to them.[63] This partly confirms Nicholas Paul's belief that the 'resonance' of the siege of Antioch 'was all the stronger because the story distinguished who stood fast in the face of danger from those who abandoned their fellows and fled back to the West'.[64] However, the anxieties and tensions which emerge in the texts suggest an even more complex picture than this, one that could have important consequences for how historians understand the interplay between crusading memory and crusade participation.[65]

Notes

1. For their invaluable insights on the ideas in this piece, I would like to thank conference audiences in Leeds and St Andrews, as well as Katy Mortimer, Beth Spacey, Stephen Spencer and Carol Sweetenham.
2. For this piece, the primary texts examined are: GF; PT; RA; FC; RM; BB; GN; AA; RC; GP. Events at Antioch were also immortalised in epic songs, wall paintings, and other forms of material culture, but these will be examined elsewhere.
3. N. Paul, *To Follow in Their Footsteps: The Crusades and Family Memory in the High Middle Ages* (Ithaca, NY, 2012); M. Cassidy-Welch (ed.), *Remembering the Crusades and Crusading* (Abingdon, 2016).
4. T. Asbridge, *The First Crusade: A New History* (London, 2004), pp. 153–240.
5. GF, pp. 28–84.
6. GF, pp. 62–3: 'Istas et multas anxietates ac angustias quas nominare nequeo passi sumus pro Christi nomine et Sancti Sepulchri via.'
7. GF, pp. 34–7 (here p. 37): 'in adiutorium Dei Sanctique Sepulchri'.
8. GF, pp. 38–41, 43–50, 56–65, 69–70, 72.
9. GF, p. 72: 'quemadmodum hunc feliciter valerent conducere et regere populum, donec peragerent iter Sancti Sepulchri, pro quo hucusque multa erant passi pericula'.
10. PT, pp. 62–114; M. G. Bull, 'The Relationship Between the *Gesta Francorum* and Peter Tudebode's *Historia de Hierosolymitano Itinere*: The Evidence of a Hitherto Unexamined Manuscript (St. Catharine's College, Cambridge, 3)', *Crusades*, 11 (2012), 1–17; RA, pp. 46–84 (here pp. 51, 53): 'flagitiorum adulterii et rapine mentes ad penitentiam concuti', 'equos suos diurna contabescere fame patiebantur.'
11. RA, pp. 55, 68: 'divina clementia eis affuit, et que lascivientes filios correxerat, nimium tristes tali modo consolata est.'
12. FC, pp. 199–203, 215–66 (here pp. 199, 222): 'De indigentia Christianorum', 'famem maximam sustinere'.
13. FC, pp. 222–6: 'illi quasi aurum ter probatum igni septiesque purgatum iamdudum a Domino praeelecti . . . et in tanta calamitate examinati, a peccatis suis mundati sunt.'
14. FC, p. 243: 'confestim cum feminis exlegibus commiscuerunt'; RA, pp. 53–4, 66 (quotation at p. 66): 'dum nostri enumerando, et recognoscendo spolia, ab oppugnatione castri superioris desisterent, atque audiendo saltatrices paganorum splendide ac superbe epularentur, nullatenus Dei memores qui tantum beneficium eis contulerat.' See also A. Holt, 'Feminine sexuality and the crusades: clerical opposition to women as a strategy for crusading success', in A. Classen (ed.), *Sexuality in the Middle Ages and Early Modern Times: New Approaches to a Fundamental Cultural-Historical and Literary-Anthropological Theme* (Berlin, 2008), pp. 449–69.
15. FC, pp. 235–41, 251–6. Raymond's stance, at least, may relate to Raymond of Toulouse's singular failure to secure material rewards in northern Syria.
16. RM, pp. 33–90; BB, pp. 37–96; GN, pp. 168–251.
17. BB, p. 43: 'Taliter autem Deus redarguebat eos misericorditer, ut ad eum toto corde conuerterentur; et si quid impenitudinis in eis latitabat, igne compunctionis et infortunio superuenientis necessitatis excocti purgarentur.'
18. BB, p. 85: 'multas passus est calamitates ut sepulcrum domini Dei sui uidere promereatur'; GN, pp. 187–8: 'assumpti huius intentionem tibi propone laboris . . . Iherosolimam deo redimere ac eius liberare Sepulchrum.'

19 GN, pp. 178, 180: 'mentis reparent vigores'.
20 GN, p. 182: 'ad dei solius subsidium, sub tanta miseria unice prestolandum, spei instinctu melioris appulsos ... quo magis suas attenderent aut copias extenuari ... eo amplius ad deum ... docerentur debita humilitate subici.'
21 GN, p. 188: 'tuam patienti Christo iam defer audaciam.'
22 RM, xlii–xlvii.
23 RM, p. 34: 'ut Dominus ostenderet oculis mortalium, quia non est virtus nec ulla potestas nisi ab ipso'.
24 RM, pp. 36–7: 'aeris inclementia, hinc misere egestatis inopia, hinc opprimebat adversariorum angustia', 'dona ... summi procuratoris'.
25 RM, p. 37: 'Sepe quidem fideles suos temptat, ut eisdem utrum diligant ipsum innotescat. Nunc temptat vos per inopie molestias, et per assiduas inimicantium vobis pressuras.'
26 RM, p. 58: 'voluit Deus ut urbs Antiochena difficulter adipisceretur, ut adepta carior haberetur.'
27 RM, p. 66: 'Omnes tribulationes et impedimenta que passi sunt ideo evenire permisi, quoniam multa nefanda operati sunt cum Christianis mulieribus et paganis, que valde displicent in oculis meis.'
28 RM, pp. 48, 53: 'nostra erit non per hominis indulgentiam, sed per celestis censure equitatem', 'Nullus nostrum pro ambitione urbis Antiochie de terra sua exivit; eam habeat cui Deus dare voluerit. Nostra omnium una sit intentio, sancti scilicet Sepulchri deliberatio.'
29 AA, pp. 182–329; GP, pp. 92–217; RC, pp. 599–716.
30 AA, pp. 206–23, 228–47, 254–63, 266–77, 284–323, 330–7.
31 AA, pp. 220, 228: 'populum Dei vivi'.
32 AA, pp. 236–8, 254–8, 274–6, 298–300, 306–8, 316.
33 AA, p. 306: 'non hunc gratis sufferre credatis laborem, sed audite et pensate premium quod Dominus Iesus omnibus hiis redditurus est qui eius amore et gratia hac in via morituri sunt.'
34 GP, pp. 98–128, 160–95.
35 GP, p. 102: 'fidei pugiles nimias penas fore viles / Corporeasque putant ... nec penis gaudia mutant / Nec bonas tormentis titubat constantia mentis, / Quamuis pressuras patiuntur corpora duras.'
36 GP, pp. 110, 160, 162, 186 (p. 160): 'per pondera tanta malorum / ... non defecisse'.
37 RC, p. 646: 'socialiter autem summi, mediocres, et imi gravia pertulerunt'. See also pp. 646–7, 650–1, 653, 659, 662–3.
38 RC, p. 663: 'igne probatum, Purgatum terrae'. See also pp. 667–71.
39 See S. Kangas, '*Deus vult*: violence and suffering as a means of salvation during the First Crusade', in T. M. S. Lehtonen, K. V. Jensen et al. (eds), *Medieval History Writing and Crusading Ideology* (Tampere, 2005), pp. 163–74; W. Purkis, *Crusading Spirituality in the Holy Land and Iberia, c. 1095–c. 1187* (Woodbridge, 2008), pp. 12–58.
40 GF, pp. 63–5, 72; RA, p. 77; FC, pp. 228, 258 (quotation at p. 258: 'factum fuit ei ad opprobrium'; PT, pp. 104–7; RM, pp. 65, 78–9; BB, pp. 74–7, 84–5; GN, pp. 227–9; GP, pp. 192–4; AA, pp. 304–6, 340–2; RC, pp. 650–1, 657–9, 687.
41 GF, pp. 32–4, 51, 63–5, 72; PT, pp 66–70, 102–3; FC, pp. 222, 228, 245–7; RA, pp. 35, 50–4, 64, 66, 68–74, 77; RM, pp. 39–41, 64–5; GN, pp. 176–85, 215–19, 227–9; BB, pp. 42–4, 66–7, 74–7, 84–5; GP, pp. 192–4; RC, pp. 656–9, 662–3.
42 *GF*, p. 32: 'vilissima omnium Christianorum'; RA, pp. 54, 68; RM, p. 41; BB, p. 66: 'ad tocius sue consanguinitatis et successionis ignominiam ignominiosiores aufugerunt'; RC, pp. 662–3.

43 GP, pp. 192-4: 'Deleo de nostro, de qualicunque libello / Hos quos non puduit sese subducere bello: / Hec miseranda cohors velut ad vomitum revocata / Pretulit exilium patrie, mundo sociata.'
44 GF, pp. 33-4, 56-7; PT, pp. 68-9, 97-8; RA, p. 74; RM, p. 40; GN, pp. 70-1, 89-90; BB, pp. 42-3, 66; AA, pp. 304, 310; RC, pp. 650-1.
45 GN, p. 217: 'nisi generis eorum amica michi contiguitate devictus pudori ipsorum parcere definissem'. See also FC, pp. 222-3, 228, 245-7; RM, pp. 64-5; GP, pp. 192-4.
46 Orderic Vitalis, *The Ecclesiastical History of Orderic Vitalis*, ed. and trans. M. Chibnall, 6 vols (Oxford, 1969-80), vol. 5, pp. 96-8; D. Roach, 'Orderic Vitalis and the First Crusade', *Journal of Medieval History*, 42/2 (2016), 177-201 (especially 185-90).
47 BB, p. 74; FC, p. 228; RM, pp. 64-5, 79; GN, pp. 102, 227-9; AA, pp. 340-2. Additionally, neither Peter Tudebode or Raymond of Aguilers comments upon Hugh's departure.
48 RM, pp. 37, 40: 'Nec mirum erat si humana fragilitas sub tot tormentis pressa murmurabat', 'tantam famis iniuriam pati nunquam didicerat.'
49 GF, pp. 34, 44, 51, 61-2 (here p. 62); FC, pp. 202, 223, 225, 228, 247, 249, 255, 263 (here p. 249): 'nostros vero milites... effici pedites, debiles, inopes'; RA, pp. 47, 49-51, 53, 55, 61, 65, 76-7; GP, pp. 104, 180; RC, pp. 646-7, 650-1, 663 (here pp. 647, 663): 'tanto tamen nobilitati asperior, quanto est durior rusticus milite, laborifer delicato', 'Qualem nulla prius sepserunt... nec post'. See also PT, pp. 65, 68, 73, 82-3, 91, 98, 102-4; RM, pp. 37, 40-1, 47, 60, 64-5, 69, 73, 76, 79; GN, pp. 174-81, 209-13, 218, 224-8; BB, pp. 38-9, 42-4, 47, 51, 55, 62, 67, 71-4, 79; AA, pp. 218-20, 228, 266-70, 288-90, 294-6, 302-6, 320, 332-4. See also J. France, *Victory in the East: A Military History of the First Crusade* (Cambridge, 1994), pp. 280-2.
50 AA, pp. 332-4: 'Super hiis miseriis et adtenuationibus nobilium procerum mirantur solummodo hii qui numquam huic simile audierunt.'
51 PT, p. 97; RC, p. 648.
52 K. A. Smith, *War and the Making of Medieval Monastic Culture* (Woodbridge, 2011), pp. 71-111.
53 S. John, 'Historical Truth and the Miraculous Past: The Use of Oral Evidence in Twelfth-Century Latin Historical Writing on the First Crusade', *English Historical Review*, 130/543 (2015), 263-301.
54 *The Chanson d'Antioche: An Old French Account of the First Crusade*, ed. and trans. C. Sweetenham and S. Edgington (Farnham, 2011), pp. 15-19.
55 C. Kostick, 'Courage and Cowardice on the First Crusade, 1096-1099', *War in History*, 20/32 (2013), 32-49; Paul, *To Follow in their Footsteps*, pp. 21-54.
56 Smith, *War and the Making of Medieval Monastic Culture*, pp. 176-9; C. Bouchard, *Strong of Body, Brave and Noble: Chivalry and Society in Medieval France* (Ithaca, NY, 1998), pp. 1-102. On the positive role such items, symbols, and networks could play, see Paul, *To Follow in their Footsteps*, pp. 55-132.
57 K. Tracy, 'Defining the medieval city through death: a case study', in A. Classen (ed.), *Urban Space in the Middle Ages and the Early Modern Age* (Berlin, 2009), pp. 183-204 (especially pp. 191-6).
58 Paul, *To Follow in their Footsteps*, pp. 134-70 (especially pp. 137-8).
59 S. A. John, '"The Feast of the Liberation of Jerusalem": Remembering and Reconstructing the First Crusade in the Holy City, 1099-1187', *Journal of Medieval History*, 41 (2015), 409-31; M. C. Gaposchkin, *Invisible Weapons: Liturgy and the Making of Crusade Ideology* (Ithaca, NY, 2017), pp. 130-91.

[60] M. Cassidy-Welch, 'Before Trauma: The Crusades, Medieval Memory and Violence', *Continuum: Journal of Media and Cultural Studies*, 31/5 (2017), 619–27 (here 626).

[61] G. Cubitt, *History and Memory* (Manchester, 2007), pp. 108–11.

[62] AA, p. 336: 'que et in obsidione urbis Antiochie mira et inaudita gesta sunt, nullius stilo, nullius memoria estimo retinenda, tot et tam diversa illic extitisse referuntur'.

[63] K. Baxter Wolff, 'Crusade and Narrative: Bohemond and the *Gesta Francorum*', *Journal of Medieval History*, 17 (1991), 207–16.

[64] Paul, *To Follow in their Footsteps*, pp. 80–3.

[65] This will be examined in a broader survey of Antioch's relationship with the crusading movement.

FRAMING THE NARRATIVE OF THE FIRST CRUSADE: THE LETTER GIVEN AT LAODICEA IN SEPTEMBER 1099[1]

Thomas W. Smith

The letter given at Laodicea (Latakia, modern Syria) in September 1099 by elements of the leadership of the First Crusade is apparently the first known written narrative of the capture of Jerusalem and, indeed, of the entire campaign, to have circulated in medieval Christendom.[2] It is, as Jay Rubenstein describes, 'a tight narrative summary of the First Crusade... [that proved to be] an extremely useful document for medieval chroniclers', and it enjoyed a widespread transmission in manuscript and rapid acceptance into universal histories.[3] Despite its status and importance to the writing of the history of the First Crusade, the agenda of the named authors in composing and structuring the account of the expedition has been little explored. The present article seeks to rectify this situation. It suggests that one of the named authors, Daibert, archbishop of Pisa and legate of Pope Urban II on the crusade, had a profound effect on the framing of the narrative of the First Crusade and its reception in the medieval West through his authorial decisions in the letter, and that, in order better to understand the reception of the crusade narrative in the high medieval West, we should attribute more attention to the letters which arose from the enterprise.[4]

The letter is addressed to 'the lord pope of the Roman Church, all the bishops and all followers of the Christian faith' ('Domino papae Romanae ecclesiae et omnibus episcopis et universis Christianae fidei cultoribus').[5] The named senders of the letter, in the order given in the text, are: 'I, the archbishop of Pisa, and other bishops and Duke Godfrey, now by the Grace of God defender of the Church of the Holy Sepulchre, Raymond, Count of St Gilles, and the entire army of God in the land of Israel' ('ego Pisanus archiepiscopus et alii episcopi et Godefridus dux, gratia Dei ecclesiae S. Sepulcri nunc aduocatus, et Raimundus comes S. Aegidii et uniuersus Dei exercitus, qui est in terra Israel').[6] The letter recounts the history of the expedition following the fall of Nicaea in June 1097, through the gruelling siege of Antioch in 1098 and the capture of Jerusalem on 15 July 1099, up to the aftermath of the Battle of Ascalon (12 August 1099) and the sojourn of the returning crusader armies at Laodicea in September 1099, where their leaders met with Daibert and Bohemond of Taranto (who were then laying siege to Laodicea) and drafted the letter.[7]

The accepted view of the composition of the letter, first argued by Heinrich Hagenmeyer in 1873 and made even more forcefully in his classic edition and study of the letters in 1901, is that despite Daibert being named first in the *salutatio*, and his use of the first-person *ego*, we should not take this to mean that he wrote the letter. Having only just arrived in the East, Hagenmeyer stated, he was not an eyewitness to the crusade and therefore could not possibly have composed such a detailed and accurate account.[8] In Hagenmeyer's view, the author (*Verfasser*) of the text was in fact none other than Raymond of Aguilers, a chaplain in the service of Raymond of St Gilles, who later composed a longer account of the crusade.[9] Hagenmeyer noticed textual similarities between the letter given at Laodicea and Raymond's *Liber* which linked the two texts and supplied a close textual comparison of relevant passages to support his argument. One clue on which he placed great emphasis was the peculiar usage of the term *Hispania* for Isfahan (rather than Spain) which appears in both texts and nowhere else in any of the Western accounts of the expedition.[10] John France also emphasised that the use of the first-person plural 'we' tallies with the Provençal experience of the campaign, and Hagenmeyer's argument has held sway ever since, albeit expressed in more cautious terms.[11] Close study of the internal contents of the letter, however, suggests an alternative interpretation.

Since Godfrey was absent at the time the letter was given, it is logical to suggest that, as the only individually named authors, Daibert and Raymond of St Gilles collaborated closely on its composition and that, although the *salutatio* pays lip-service to the *alii episcopi* and the *uniuersus Dei exercitus, qui est in terra Israel*, they were the two driving forces behind the document's issue. This is the view taken most recently by Susan Edgington, who states that the author was Daibert, who 'wrote it as if from himself and Count Raymond, who was alongside him in Latakia, and Duke Godfrey, who was not there but in Jerusalem'.[12] Raymond of St Gilles and Daibert were, after all, connected through Urban II's preparations for the crusade, and the archbishop spent time with the count after his arrival in the East, so their collaboration should perhaps come as little surprise.[13] As noted by Hagenmeyer, the newly arrived archbishop did not take part in the crusade campaign proper and he would have been reliant upon veteran crusaders for his account of the crusade. It follows that the narrative core of the missive is received from Raymond and his contingent, something apparently confirmed by the espousal of the Provençal perspective on the campaign and the assertion of the authenticity of the Holy Lance in particular.[14] The principal contributions of this article are that, while such Provençal influence on the letter can be felt via Raymond of St Gilles, the internal evidence of the text suggests that we should attribute a more significant and dynamic authorial role in framing the narrative to Daibert, who deliberately shaped its content in order to assert his authority in the East and propound an ecclesiastical narrative of the First Crusade, in what is the first written account of the whole campaign known to have circulated in the West. If Raymond of Aguilers did indeed draft the text, he appears to have done so at the direction of Daibert.

We begin with the most obvious point in favour of the notion that Daibert had the greatest influence over the composition of the letter, and, correspondingly, the clue most vociferously rejected by Hagenmeyer: the order of the *intitulatio* in the greeting clause. Daibert is accorded pride of place as the first named author. The other bishops (*alii episcopi*) are also named before the (absent) *aduocatus* of Jerusalem, Godfrey of Bouillon, who is relegated to third place, followed by Raymond of St Gilles, and then the rest of the army (*universus Dei exercitus*).[15] As Nicholas Vincent so convincingly demonstrates, the order of episcopal witnesses in medieval charters could be a source of great contention.[16] Similarly the contemporary rules of diplomatic were clear that the ordering of senders and recipients in the *salutatio* should be determined by status.[17] According to the norms of contemporary diplomatic and documentary cultures, then, Daibert was positioning himself as the foremost figure among the senders specifically, especially with his use of the first-person form *ego* to emphasise his personal role, and also probably staking claims for the precedence of the episcopate generally, although apparently none of the *alii episcopi* were important enough or played a significant enough role in the issue of the letter to warrant mention by name. It follows that Daibert probably had the greatest influence over the issue of the letter, and, by extension, that he controlled the drafting process, even if the source of much of the account of the crusade came from Raymond and the act of writing the text itself was performed by one of their chaplains, such as Raymond of Aguilers. Raymond of St Gilles was probably pushing for recognition throughout Christendom as one of the foremost leaders by being named in the *intitulatio* and also seeking to promote the Provençal perspective in retelling the course of the crusade. Although he had only just arrived in the East and missed almost the entire crusade, Daibert, for his part, appears to have been angling to be recognised as the ecclesiastical leader of the crusaders.

Why did Daibert seek to assert his precedence over the crusader host in the composition and despatch of the letter? *Cui bono* – who benefited? The purpose of the letter was multifaceted. Its basic function is obvious: to inform the faithful of the West what had happened in the East, but there were two complementary agendas at play. One purpose was to invite the pope and all Christians in the West to celebrate the success of the expedition and its participants, as the final section of the first recension of the letter states: 'And so we call on you, [and] all the bishops, devout clerics, monks and all the laity, to glory in the marvellous bravery and devotion of our brothers' ('ad tam mirabilem fratrum nostrorum fortitudinis deuotionem . . . inuitamus uos exsultationem et omnes episcopos et bonae uitae clericos, monachosque et omnes laicos').[18] The association of the crusaders with this endeavour within the text, and especially those named in the *intitulatio* as the bearers of the news, immortalised them in the process. This is, indeed, exactly how the letter was received. Very soon after entering transmission in Europe (we know that Count Robert of Flanders was one of the returning veterans who carried and spread the letter, and presumably others did too),[19] the document acquired two postscripts: one calling upon those in the West to pay the debts of returning survivors in return for a share of their spiritual reward, and the other supplying a short summary of the dates of landmark battles, almost certainly to facilitate liturgical celebration.[20] An important manuscript witness now preserved in Würzburg bears a unique rhymed Latin inscription at the head of its copy of the text calling upon readers (and listeners) to meditate upon the crusade, using the letter as a way of magnifying the glory of the event.[21] Connected to this was the need to recruit new warrior-pilgrims for the defence of the city of Jerusalem, and this letter and others – such as Daibert's letter to the people of Germany, given as patriarch of Jerusalem in April 1100 – clearly whipped up enthusiasm and its extended manuscript transmission in Germany can probably be connected to recruitment for the Crusade of 1100–1.[22]

Reading between the lines there was also a more worldly and pragmatic agenda at play. By adopting a leading role in the control and transmission of information, and by sending this official report (*offizieller Bericht*) back to the pope, Daibert was also staking his claim to ecclesiastical authority in the East.[23] As Michael Matzke convincingly argues, Pope Urban II had sent Daibert on the crusade as his legate to play a leading role in the expedition and its ecclesiastical affairs.[24] Daibert's connection to Raymond may have been part of an attempt to position himself as the direct successor to the previous papal legate, Adhémar of Le Puy, whose memory quickly assumed importance in the crusade narrative, and to benefit from the prominent leadership role that his predecessor had played. It should not be seen as peculiar that Daibert did not give the title of legate along with that of archbishop of Pisa in the *intitulatio* of the letter, however. He was clearly aware of the death of Urban but not the election of Paschal II, which explains why the letter is addressed *Domino papae Romanae ecclesiae* without specifying a pontifical name. Apparently Daibert considered his legatine mandate to have lapsed along with the death of Urban, although in the twelfth century there was no consensus on whether the death of a pope revoked his legatine mandates.[25] The formulation of an official report was, as Matzke writes, in accordance with Daibert's responsibilities as papal representative, and should probably be read as an attempt to take control over, or at least been seen as a leader of, the crusader army.[26] Even if Daibert had technically lost his legatine power, he proceeded to throw his weight around in the East in a manner commensurate with his earlier authority, and the letter fits into a pattern of assertive behaviour.[27] When he arrived in Jerusalem at Christmas 1099, he succeeded in having his authority recognised by quashing the election of Arnulf of Choques as patriarch of Jerusalem and having himself elected in Arnulf's place only six days after his arrival.[28] The Laodicea letter, in which Daibert assumes and consciously displays precedence, should probably be interpreted as part of his machinations to have his authority recognised in the East. Finally, there is another, more subtle function of the issue of the letter which the second part of this article will explore: the framing of the narrative of the First Crusade.

Having only just arrived in the Holy Land, and with no personal experience of the crusade proper, Daibert had to decide where the narrative of the crusade should begin in framing the letter. After an extremely brief *arenga*, which provided only the most basic theological context for the success of the crusade, stating that the letter's audience should 'Multiply prayers and invocations with joy and exultation in the sight of the Lord since God has magnified his mercy by fulfilling through us what he had promised in ancient times' ('Multiplicate preces et orationes cum iocunditate et exsultatione in conspectu Domini, quoniam Deus magnificauit misericordiam suam complendo in nobis ea, quae antiquis temporibus promiserat'), Daibert chose the fall of Nicaea on 19 June 1097 to demarcate the beginning of his narrative: 'After the capture of Nicaea . . .' ('etenim cum capta Nicaea . . .').[29] Daibert's authorial choice here is perhaps significant, since it delineates his conception of the chronological framing of the crusade. Other letters from the leaders had already informed the papacy about the course of the expedition at least up until 11 September 1098, when the princes sent a missive to Urban II (and it is likely that others were despatched thereafter which no longer survive).[30] The selection of the aftermath of Nicaea for the beginning of the letter therefore was not a logical continuation of the crusader princes' previous correspondence with the papacy, but a deliberate decision in framing the narrative. This, according to Daibert, and perhaps Raymond of St Gilles (who must have been feeding the archbishop the information necessary to write the letter), was where the campaign of the crusade proper began. Of course, the epistolary form in which Daibert and Raymond chose to communicate dictated that the text be brief, but it is perhaps significant that they chose not to recount any of the events in Europe or Byzantium, and that the narrative concerns only Latin conquests in the East. Because Nicaea was surrendered to the Byzantines apparently it was of lesser priority.[31] Interestingly, this framing aligns with modern historians' structuring of the phases of the expedition. For Jonathan Riley-Smith, the first phase 'stretched from western Europe to Nicaea'.[32] The evidence from the letter demonstrates that some medieval observers also conceptualised the enterprise in a strikingly similar manner.

Study of the epistle's reception reveals that this chronological framing of the First Crusade resonated with its audience. If we turn to the second postscript (appended to the main text of the *epistula* in its third recension), which supplements Daibert's narrative in the main body of the letter with a compressed compilation of the dates of all the major battles of the crusade, we find that readers of the document broadly followed Daibert's lead in conceptualising the course of the main campaign. This list of dates also contains only events which occurred in the East, though it extends the narrative backwards slightly to 'the first battle, in which many Turks were killed, [which] was at the bridge on the River Farfar on the ninth day before the kalends of March' ('primum eorum bellum fuit apud pontem Farfar fluminis, in quo multi Turcorum interfecti sunt IX Kalendis Martii').[33] The next significant engagement, however, the 'second battle, a Christian victory over the pagans was at Nicaea on the third day before the nones of March' ('Secundum bellum fuit apud Nicaeam III Nonis Martii, in quo pagani a Christianis uicti sunt'), brings the rest of the chronology into line with that of Daibert in the main body of the text.[34] Shifting our perspective on the chronological framing also explains why the postscript seems to misdate the capture of the Jerusalem to 'the third year of their expedition' ('anno III profectionis eorum'), a chronological quirk which appears to be a simple mistake and the result of deficient knowledge on the part of the scribe who first compiled the summary, which is littered with incorrect dates.[35] This apparent mistake is perhaps not a result of misdating, but the product of the reception of Daibert's framing of the history, which, for him and apparently for many of those who read his letter, properly began in the East, in the first half of 1097. If we adopt this altered chronological framework and count forwards from the 'first battle' in March 1097, or even the fall of Nicaea in June of that year, then the conquest of Jerusalem on 15 July 1099 did indeed fall in the third year of the expedition. This suggests that Daibert's framing of the narrative of the First Crusade did influence contemporary ideas about the chronology of the crusade, and that the significance of the document in the reception of the crusade narrative in the West has been underestimated.

Daibert also influenced the reception of the crusade narrative through his ecclesiastical framing, and, in some ways, the narrative in the letter aligns with the longer accounts composed in the following decade. As Gerd Althoff notes, it is similar to other accounts of the crusade which emphasise God's help in return for liturgical supplication by the pilgrims.[36] The theology of the letter is conventional in its exposition of God's role in the expedition. It relates that God deliberately placed challenges in the way of army, most notably the gruelling siege of Antioch, explaining that 'because [earlier] successes bred arrogance among some of us, God placed Antioch in our path ... There he detained us for nine months and during the siege so humbled us that eventually all our pride and arrogance turned to humility' ('ob haec itaque feliciter acta, quia quidem intumuerant, opposuit nobis Deus Antiochiam ... ibique per IX menses nos detinuit atque in obsidione extra ita humiliauit, donec omnis superbiae nostrae tumor in humilitatem recurrit').[37] After adopting humility befitting their status as pilgrims and showing due devotion to the Lord, God rewarded the crusaders with the fall of the city. As Andrew D. Buck demonstrates, such ideas were incorporated into longer narratives as divine tests of the piety of the crusaders, and as a mode of theological interpretation it is ubiquitous in contemporary histories of the crusade, especially on the subject of the siege of Antioch.[38] It is most likely that this represents the prevailing view among the crusader host, rather than the influence of Daibert's letter alone, although this surely played a role given the large number of known manuscript witnesses (which currently stands at twenty-one copies) and its inclusion in universal histories and letter collections such as the *Codex Udalrici*.[39] We can point to one account of a miracle in the letter, an indication of God's favour before the Battle of Ascalon, which seems to have influenced later narratives. Immediately before the battle, thousands of captured animals formed themselves into columns and 'when the people advanced in battle order the camels, oxen and sheep advanced in similar formations with us, stopping when we stopped, going forward when we did and running when we ran' ('haec autem animalia nobiscum comitabantur, ut cum stantibus starent, cum procedentibus procederent, cum currentibus currerent').[40] On this point Raymond of Aguilers's *Liber* matches the letter exactly and must have used it as a source: 'ut starent cum stantibus cum currentibus currerent, cum procedentibus, procederent'.[41] Fulcher of Chartres also recounts the miracle in similar terms and it may be that he received this information through Daibert's letter.[42] In turn, Fulcher's text was received by William of Malmesbury, reinforcing the place of this miracle in the crusade narrative.[43]

Perhaps most notable from the document's otherwise fairly standard theological mode of exposition is that there is no mention of the deeds of individual crusaders or contingents and almost no mention of any tactical or strategic decisions, aspects which are staples of the longer narratives. Instead, all the military successes, especially the capture of Antioch and Jerusalem, but also the Battle of Ascalon, are attributed to the penitential acts of a united army alone. The letter pastes over cracks in the unity of the host, passing over the desertions at Antioch and stating that the army was not many, but unanimous and united in its desire to reach Jerusalem: 'our army was not large and everyone was in a hurry to get to Jerusalem' ('exercitus noster non multus erat, et in Hierusalem unanimiter uenire festinabant').[44] The most detailed account of a military engagement is that of the action at the Battle of Ascalon in August 1099, which includes more detailed strategic information and a record of the martial deeds of the army as a whole than in the preceding sections – though no individuals or contingents are picked out and the collective deeds are tempered by the providential interpretation. When the crusaders 'caught sight of our enemy we went down on our knees to ask God for His help' ('cumque exercitus noster et hostium se conspexissent, genibus flexis adiutorem Deum inuocauimus').[45] The size of the crusader host is given in precise terms, 'five thousand knights and fifteen thousand foot-soldiers' ('V milia militum et XV milia peditum'), in comparison to their Egyptian foes, who commanded 'a hundred thousand horsemen and four hundred thousand foot-soldiers' ('C milia equitum et CCCC milia peditum').[46] As is well known, the portrayal of a small army against a superior foe was meant to align the crusaders with the biblical armies from the Old Testament, and is an interpretation standard for high medieval crusade texts.[47] This is also where the reader first receives information about the collective martial deeds of the army, such as how many enemies were killed and how, which diverges from the purely ecclesiastical framing of the rest of the campaign:

> [God] caused our mere rush to rout this multitude and scatter all their weapons, so that even if they had wanted to fight back afterwards they would not have had the means to do so . . . More than one hundred thousand Moors fell beneath the sword, while the panic was so great that up to 2,000 were suffocated in the crush at the city gate. There are no figures however for those who drowned in the sea. Many were caught in the thickets.
> pro solo impetu nostro hanc in fugam multitudinem uertit et omnia arma eorum diripuit, ut, si deinceps nobis repugnare uellent, nec haberent arma, in quibus sperarent . . . ceciderunt ibi plus quam C milia Maurorum gladio. Timor autem eorum tantus erat, ut in porta ciuitatis ad II milia suffocati sint. De his uero, qui in mari interierunt, non est numerus. Spineta etiam ex ipsis multos obtinuerunt.[48]

In portraying the crusader host as a united and deeply religious army, the letter presages the later Benedictine rewritings of the history of the First Crusade in which Robert the Monk, Guibert of Nogent and Baldric of Bourgueil 'put the miracle, as they saw it, of the success of the crusade into the context of providential history and they chose to treat the crusaders as temporary religious, professed into what looked to them like a military monastery on the move.[49] What is noteworthy about the letter is that the text always presents a united host and does not pick out any particular warriors or contingents for special praise, as later accounts do.

That said, it must be remembered, of course, that the letter presents the Provençal perspective of the campaign, asserting, for example, the authenticity of the Holy Lance: at Antioch, God 'showed us His lance, which had not been seen since the time of the Apostles' ('lanceam suam ... non uisum a tempore apostolorum ... nobis obtulit').[50] But despite the supposedly key role in composition played by Raymond of St Gilles, none of his personal crusading deeds are recorded, nor are those of any other crusaders in the manner that Raymond of Aguilers does in his *Liber*.[51] If the count of St Gilles's scribe really did have such influence over the composition of the text down to the spelling *Hispania*, we would expect to find something of Raymond's deeds. Rather, we find the bishops in the army playing a leading role. At the beginning of the siege of Jerusalem, which opened with a barefoot procession around its walls performed by the penitent crusaders, it is noteworthy that the bishops precede the princes in the leadership of army and that the key to the fall of Jerusalem was a display of religiosity rather than martial superiority:

> at a meeting of a council the bishops and princes decided that we should go barefooted around the outside of the city ... Eight days after our act of humility the Lord showed He was placated by delivering to us the city and His enemies.
> habito consilio, episcopi et principes circinandam esse ciuitatem nudis pedibus praedicauerunt ... placatus itaque hac humilitate Dominus, VIII° die post humiliationem nostram ciuitatem cum suis hostibus nobis tribuit.[52]

The promotion of episcopal authority within the leadership of the crusader host in this passage fits with Daibert's agenda to assert ecclesiastical authority over the crusade, and, specifically, to extend his own power. That the success of the crusade is framed in such theological terms, with no mention made of the martial deeds of individual crusaders, is another indicator that Daibert took the lead in crafting the letter, and not Raymond of St Gilles or his chaplain and namesake.

Famously, the bloodshed during the capture of Jerusalem is described in the letter in a chillingly laconic fashion: 'Should you wish to learn what happened to the enemies we found inside [Jerusalem], know that our horsemen rode knee-deep in Saracen blood in Solomon's Porch and in his Temple' ('et si scire desideratis, quid de hostibus ibi repertis factum fuerit, scitote: quia in porticu Salomonis et in templo eius nostri equitabant in sanguine Saracenorum usque ad genua equorum').[53] Althoff uses the letter as a *Schlüsselzeugnis* (key testimony) for his interpretation of the Church's attitude towards violence in the Middle Ages because, he claims, it is not an attempt to fashion a later justification for the violence that occurred during the capture of Jerusalem, but an eyewitness account composed with the understanding that the recipient of the letter, the pope (whom Althoff names as Urban II, but who, as we have noted, was already dead, and whose death was known to Daibert), would be in accord with the account of that violence.[54] As noted above, having only just arrived in the East after the conquest of the Holy Land, Daibert was not an eyewitness, Godfrey was absent, and as the present article argues, the archbishop was consciously framing an ecclesiastical narrative of the crusade. Although this does not affect Althoff's argument that the expression of the violence would have been in accord with what the papal curia expected, we should be very wary of accepting the letter as the testimony of the crusaders themselves since it was written by a member of that very curia *in provincia*. Because Daibert refashioned the crusaders' accounts through an ecclesiastical filter, we cannot use the letter as evidence of how strongly their understanding of the expedition was 'under the influence of ecclesiastical arguments' ('wie sehr die Kreuzfahrer unter dem Eindruck christlich kirchlicher Argumente standen'); instead, it should be treated like the other narratives of the crusade which were also composed according to authorial agendas.[55]

Perhaps the most surprising (and interesting) thing about the epistle is the focus (or, better, foci) of its content and how little space is dedicated to the conquest of Jerusalem, which extends little further than the two quotations provided above. The account of the siege of Jerusalem and its capture is surprisingly brief for such a momentous event – at least according to what the general scholarly consensus has conditioned us to expect was the focal point of the crusade. As Georg Strack argues, the status of Jerusalem as the main goal of the expedition is not quite as clear-cut as many scholars suggest.[56] In fact, the letter text dwells much longer on the siege of Antioch and the Battle of Ascalon – the fall of Jerusalem is little more than an interlude between the two. This reflects the actual length of the siege at Antioch and the more harrowing tribulations of the army there, and it is interesting to note that the heavy focus on Antioch in the letter is reflected in the later, longer narratives of the crusade. As explored above, there is also a noticeable shift in content, framing and level of detail in the letter's account of the action at Ascalon. Is it possible that Daibert's sources were able to offer more detail on this most recent engagement? Hagenmeyer, for instance, argued that the uneven length of the coverage of events in the letter, which strongly privileges the Battle of Ascalon, results from the fact that this event was the most recent and was therefore fresh in the memory.[57] The main point, though, is that Jerusalem and the Holy Sepulchre are not in any way the central, or even *a* central, focus in the body of the letter (indeed, the only mention of the Holy Sepulchre is Godfrey's title as *aduocatus* of the tomb in the *salutatio*), even though, as we have seen, its author fashions the crusade narrative into an ecclesiastical account. This apparent lack of interest in Jerusalem and the Holy Sepulchre renders the Laodicea letter out of step with the narratives composed in the following decade in the West and the modern scholarly consensus on Jerusalem as the single most important goal of the crusade.[58]

This lack of focus on Jerusalem changes, however, when we turn from the composition of the text in the East to examine the letter's reception in the West. The second postscript, which compiles in the third recension a compressed list of key battle dates for liturgical celebration, mentions Jerusalem twice. It is foregrounded in the opening of the addendum: 'Jerusalem was captured by the Christians in the year of the Lord 1099, on the Ides of July, 6th feria in the seventh indiction, in the third year of their expedition' ('Capta est autem Hierusalem a Christianis anno Domini MXCIX, Idus Iulii, feriae VI, indictione VII, anno III profectionis eorum'), and noted again towards its conclusion: 'Their fifth battle was on the Ides of July when Jerusalem was captured after thirty-nine days of siege' ('quintum eorum bellum fuit Idibus Iulii, quando post tricesimum nonum obsidionis diem capta est Hierusalem').[59] The European reception of the letter, then, while accepting the basic narrative framing of the campaign in the East, placed much more emphasis on the capture of Jerusalem than Daibert himself did. This is consistent with the shaping of the history of the crusade in the West after 1099, when Jerusalem and the Holy Sepulchre became the focal points of the entire enterprise in the Benedictine rewritings of the *Gesta Francorum*. That Daibert's letter bucks this trend and offers a distinct narrative focus is significant.

In conclusion, the letter given at Laodicea in September 1099 can no longer be used as an unfiltered eyewitness account of the First Crusade. As this article has revealed, rather than attributing the authorship to Raymond of Aguilers on behalf of Raymond of St Gilles, as Hagenmeyer argued, the author dictating the content of the text must, in fact, have been Daibert, archbishop of Pisa. The letter hardly lacks an agenda. Raymond of St Gilles succeeded in cementing his position in the very top tier of the leadership of the crusade and ensured that it was the Provençal account of events that was recognised as the 'official' one in the report of the (former) papal legate. Daibert, for his part, styled himself as the foremost leader of the enterprise in his attempt to assert his ecclesiastical authority and seize power in the East – which he did, very successfully, when he had himself installed as patriarch of Jerusalem a few months later. In so doing, Daibert framed the first written Latin narrative of the whole campaign of the First Crusade known to have circulated in the West. While the theological interpretation of successes and setbacks being the work of God, who was testing the faith of the pilgrims, is entirely conventional, the framing of the letter is significant for three main reasons. First, in setting a distinct chronological framework for the campaign proper which began only with the Latin conquests after Nicaea. Second, in devoting much more attention to Antioch and the Battle of Ascalon than the capture of Jerusalem and the Holy Sepulchre, which later became the ultimate focal points of the crusade narrative in the West in the following decade. And third, in using the document as a vehicle for an ecclesiastical narrative that did not mention the deeds of individual crusaders or contingents at all, but instead promoted the authority and role of the episcopate in the leadership of the crusade.

Notes

[1] I am very grateful to the Leverhulme Trust for the award of an Early Career Fellowship, held at the University of Leeds (2017–20), during which this article was written. My thanks to Andrew D. Buck for his comments on the article and to Georg Strack for a helpful conversation on the topic.

[2] Kb, no. XVIII, pp. 167–74; the *Codex Udalrici* version of the letter has been recently edited in *Codex Udalrici*, ed. K. Nass, 2 vols, MGH Die Briefe der deutschen Kaiserzeit, 10 (Wiesbaden, 2017), vol. 2, no. 259, pp. 449–53; the letter is translated in M. Barber and K. Bate (trans.), *Letters from the East: Crusaders, Pilgrims and Settlers in the 12th–13th Centuries*, Crusade Texts in Translation, 18 (Farnham, 2010) (henceforth *Letters*), pp. 33–7. See: T. W.

Smith, 'The First Crusade Letter Written at Laodicea in 1099: Two Previously Unpublished Versions from Munich, Bayerische Staatsbiblitohek Clm 23390 and 28195', *Crusades*, 15 (2016), 1–25; T. W. Smith, 'Scribal Crusading: Three New Manuscript Witnesses to the Regional Reception and Transmission of First Crusade Letters', *Traditio*, 72 (2017), 133–69; Hagenmeyer's extremely detailed commentary on the letter is in Kb, pp. 371–403, and his assessment of the manuscript traditions (now superseded by Smith, 'First Crusade Letter' and 'Scribal Crusading') is at pp. 103–14; H. Hagenmeyer, 'Der Brief der Kreuzfahrer an den Pabst und die abenländische Kirche v. J. 1099 nach der Schlacht bei Askalon', *Forschungen zur deutschen Geschichte*, 13 (1873), 400–12; P. Riant, 'Inventaire critique des lettres historiques des croisades', *Archives de l'Orient latin*, 1 (1880), 1–235 (here 201–4); and also T. J. H. McCarthy, *The Continuations of Frutolf of Michelsberg's Chronicle*, MGH Schriften, 74 (Wiesbaden, 2018), pp. 88 and n. 18, 146–9, 192–5, 202; J. France, 'The Anonymous *Gesta Francorum* and the *Historia Francorum qui ceperunt Iherusalem* of Raymond of Aguilers and the *Historia de Hierosolymitano itinere* of Peter Tudebode: An Analysis of the Textual Relationship between Primary Sources for the First Crusade', in J. France and W. G. Zajac (eds), *The Crusades and their Sources: Essays Presented to Bernard Hamilton* (Aldershot, 1998), pp. 39–69 (here pp. 42–3); J. Riley-Smith, 'The Title of Godfrey of Bouillon', *Bulletin of the Institute of Historical Research*, 52 (1979), 83–6 (here 84); A. V. Murray, *The Crusader Kingdom of Jerusalem: A Dynastic History, 1099–1125* (Oxford, 2000), p. 71.

3   J. Rubenstein, 'Holy Fire and Sacral Kingship in Post-Conquest Jerusalem', *Journal of Medieval History*, 43/4 (2017), 470–84 (here 475). See also Kb, p. 107. On the manuscript transmission, see Smith, 'Scribal Crusading' and Smith, 'First Crusade Letter'. On the acceptance of the letter into the continuations of Frutolf, for example, see McCarthy, *The Continuations of Frutolf*, pp. 88, 146–9, 192–5, 202.

4   On the narrative of the First Crusade and its reception in the West, in addition to the introductions to AA, BB and RM, see most recently: S. T. Parsons, 'The Letters of Stephen of Blois Reconsidered', *Crusades*, 17 (2018), 1–29; C. Symes, 'Popular Literacies and the First Historians of the First Crusade', *Past and Present*, 235 (2017), 37–67; E. Lapina, *Warfare and the Miraculous in the Chronicles of the First Crusade* (University Park, PA, 2015); S. John, 'Historical Truth and the Miraculous Past: The Use of Oral Evidence in Twelfth-Century Latin Historical Writing on the First Crusade', *English Historical Review*, 130 (2015), 263–301; M. Bull and D. Kempf (eds), *Writing the Early Crusades: Text, Transmission and Memory* (Woodbridge, 2014); M. Bull, 'The Historiographical Construction of a Northern French First Crusade', *Haskins Society Journal*, 25 (2013), 35–56; M. Bull, 'The Western Narratives of the First Crusade', in D. Thomas and A. Mallett (eds), *Christian–Muslim Relations: A Bibliographical History*, Volume 3: *1050–1200* (Leiden, 2011), pp. 15–25; N. L. Paul, 'A Warlord's Wisdom: Literacy and Propaganda at the Time of the First Crusade', *Speculum*, 85 (2010), 534–66; J. Flori, *Chroniqueurs et propagandistes: Introduction critique aux sources de la première croisade* (Geneva, 2010); J. Rubenstein, 'What is the *Gesta Francorum*, and Who was Peter Tudebode?', *Revue Mabillon*, n.s., 77/16 (2005), 179–204; J. Rubenstein, 'Putting History to Use: Three Crusade Chronicles in Context', *Viator*, 35 (2004), 131–68.

5   Kb, p. 168; trans. *Letters*, p. 34.
6   Kb, p. 168; trans. *Letters*, p. 34.
7   See M. Matzke, *Daibert von Pisa: Zwischen Pisa, Papst und erstem Kreuzzug* (Sigmaringen, 1998), pp. 150–1.
8   Kb, p. 108: 'Die Epistula beginnt zwar Abs[atz] 1 mit den Worten "Pisanus archiepiscopus et alii episcopi" etc, hieraus darf aber keineswegs gefolgert werden, weil Dagobert zuerst genannt ist und im Falle auch das "ego" vor "Pisanus archiep[iscopus]" authentisch

sein sollte, weil er sich in dieser Weise einführt, dass er auch der Briefschreiber gewesen sei, denn er wäre wohl nicht im Stande gewesen, da er ja nicht Augenzeuge des darin Berichteten und erst gegen September 1099 nach Palästina gekommen war, einen so zutreffenden Bericht zu erstatten.'

9 Hagenmeyer, 'Der Brief der Kreuzfahrer', 405–10; Kb, pp. 108–10. Raymond's account is printed in RA. I am preparing a new monograph study *The Letters of the First Crusade* for the series Crusading in Context, forthcoming with The Boydell Press.

10 Hagenmeyer, 'Der Brief der Kreuzfahrer', 407.

11 Kb, p. 106; France, 'The Anonymous *Gesta Francorum*', pp. 42–3; Smith, 'First Crusade Letter', 3–4; Rubenstein, 'Holy Fire and Sacral Kingship', 475; Riley-Smith, 'The Title of Godfrey of Bouillon', 84.

12 S. B. Edgington, *Baldwin I of Jerusalem, 1100–1118* (Abingdon, 2019), p. 62.

13 Matzke, *Daibert von Pisa*, pp. 107, 151, 166; Murray, *Crusader Kingdom*, p. 81; S. John, *Godfrey of Bouillon: Duke of Lower Lotharingia, Ruler of Latin Jerusalem, c. 1060–1100* (Abingdon, 2018), p. 199.

14 On the Holy Lance, see J. Riley-Smith, *The First Crusade and the Idea of Crusading* (London, 1986), pp. 95–8.

15 On Godfrey's absence and the title *aduocatus*, see: John, *Godfrey of Bouillon*, pp. 180–90; Edgington, *Baldwin I*, pp. 62–3; Hagenmeyer, 'Der Brief der Kreuzfahrer', 401; Riley-Smith, 'The Title of Godfrey of Bouillon'; Murray, *Crusader Kingdom*, p. 71; Smith, 'First Crusade Letter', 3.

16 N. Vincent, 'Shall the first be last? Order and disorder amongst Henry II's Bishops', in T. W. Smith (ed.), *Authority and Power in the Medieval Church, c. 1000–c. 1500* (Turnhout, forthcoming).

17 See, for example, P. Chaplais, *English Diplomatic Practice* (London, 2003), pp. 102–3.

18 Kb, p. 173; trans. *Letters*, p. 36.

19 McCarthy, *The Continuations of Frutolf*, p. 88 and n. 18; G. Waitz (ed.), MGH *Scriptores*, vol. 6 (Hanover, 1844), p. 216.

20 Kb, pp. 173–4. On the different recensions, including the identification of a fourth recension unknown to Hagenmeyer, see Smith, 'First Crusade Letter'.

21 Würzburg, Universitätsbibliothek Würzburg, M. p. th. q. 17, fol. 90r: 'Hec qui scire sitis lege de Iherosolimitis / Multiplicant laudes rem si gestam bene gaudes.' See Smith, 'Scribal Crusading', esp. 133.

22 Smith, 'Scribal Crusading', 134, 148–9. On Daibert's letter of April 1100 see Smith, 'Scribal Crusading', 134, 148–9, and for a new, critical edition 168–9.

23 I am grateful to Georg Strack for advice on this point.

24 Matzke, *Daibert von Pisa*, pp. 135–41; Murray, *Crusader Kingdom*, p. 82 and n. 88.

25 Kb, pp. 106–7; Matzke, *Daibert von Pisa*, pp. 139–40, 141, 151; John, *Godfrey of Bouillon*, p. 199. See also P. Skinner, 'From Pisa to the Patriarchate: Chapters in the Life of (Arch)Bishop Daibert', in P. Skinner (ed.), *Challenging the Boundaries of Medieval History: The Legacy of Timothy Reuter* (Turnhout, 2009), pp. 155–72 (here p. 164) on this point.

26 Matzke, *Daibert von Pisa*, p. 141 gives it as one of Daibert's responsibilities after arriving in the East, which Matzke explains as 'die Übermittlung des päpstlichen Grußes und Segens sowie die Abfassung eines offiziellen Berichtes der Kreuzfahrer an den noch unbekannten Papst [Urban II had died in the meantime] und die westliche Christenheit'.

27 A. V. Murray, 'Review of Michael Matzke, *Daibert von Pisa: Zwischen Pisa, Papst und erstem Kreuzzug*', *Speculum*, 78/3 (2003), 954–6 (here 955); Skinner, 'From Pisa to the Patriarchate', p. 164.

28 Matzke, *Daibert von Pisa*, pp. 153–66 (esp. p. 166); Murray, *Crusader Kingdom*, pp. 182–3; Rubenstein, 'Holy Fire and Sacral Kingship', 475; John, *Godfrey of Bouillon*, pp. 199–200.
29 Kb, p. 168; trans. *Letters*, p. 34.
30 Kb, no. XVI, pp. 161–5.
31 Riley-Smith, *The First Crusade*, p. 58.
32 Riley-Smith, *The First Crusade*, p. 64.
33 Kb, p. 174; trans. *Letters*, p. 36.
34 Kb, p. 174; trans. *Letters*, p. 36.
35 Kb, p. 174; trans. *Letters*, p. 36. The errors in dating events in the postscript are discussed in Kb, p. 402.
36 G. Althoff, *'Selig sind, die Verfolgung ausüben': Päpste und Gewalt im Hochmittelalter* (Stuttgart, 2013), pp. 138–9.
37 Kb, p. 169; trans. *Letters*, p. 34.
38 Andrew D. Buck in this volume.
39 Smith, 'Scribal Crusading', 141, 157–61; Kb, p. 107; McCarthy, *The Continuations of Frutolf*, pp. 88, 146–9, 192–5, 202; *Codex Udalrici*, ed. Nass, vol. 2, no. 259, pp. 449–53.
40 Kb, pp. 172–3; trans. *Letters*, p. 36. On miracles and the crusades, see Lapina, *Warfare and the Miraculous* and B. C. Spacey, *The Miraculous and the Writing of Crusade History* (Woodbridge, forthcoming).
41 RA, p. 158.
42 FC, pp. 313–14.
43 WM, vol. 1, p. 653; see Lapina, *Warfare and the Miraculous*, pp. 24–5.
44 Kb, p. 170; trans. *Letters*, p. 35.
45 Kb, p. 171; trans. *Letters*, p. 35.
46 Kb, p. 172; trans. *Letters*, p. 35.
47 See, for example, E. Lapina and N. Morton (eds), *The Uses of the Bible in Crusader Sources* (Leiden, 2017).
48 Kb, p. 172; trans. *Letters*, pp. 35–6.
49 Riley-Smith, *The First Crusade*, p. 2. See also W. J. Purkis, *Crusading Spirituality in the Holy Land and Iberia, c. 1095–c. 1187* (Woodbridge, 2008).
50 Kb, p. 170; trans. *Letters*, p. 34.
51 RA, *passim*. On Raymond, see T. Lecaque, *Raymond of Saint-Gilles: Occitanian Culture and Piety in the Time of the First Crusade* (Abingdon, forthcoming).
52 Kb, pp. 170–1; trans. *Letters*, p. 35.
53 Kb, p. 171; trans. *Letters*, p. 35. On this, see L. Russo, 'The Sack of Jerusalem in 1099 and Crusader Violence Viewed by Contemporary Chroniclers', in Lapina and Morton (eds), *Uses of the Bible in Crusader Sources*, pp. 63–73 (here pp. 69–70); T. F. Madden, 'Rivers of Blood: An Analysis of One Aspect of the Crusader Conquest of Jerusalem in 1099', *Revista Chilena de Estudios Medievales*, 1 (2012), 25–37; B. Z. Kedar, 'The Jerusalem Massacre of July 1099 in the Western Historiography of the Crusades', *Crusades*, 3 (2004), 15–75 (esp. 18); J. Rubenstein, *Armies of Heaven: The First Crusade and the Quest for Apocalype* (New York, 2011), pp. 286–92.
54 Althoff, *Päpste und Gewalt im Hochmittelalter*, p. 137: 'Da der Brief ein Schlüsselzeugnis für meine Interpretation darstellt . . . Er ist deshalb ein Schlüsselzeugnis, weil er nicht ein Versuch nachträglicher Rechtfertigung des Geschehens ist, sondern ganz augenscheinlich von den Ausstellern im Bewusstsein verfasst wurde, dass ihre Taten – und auch das Vorgehen in Jerusalem – mit den Vorgaben und Vorstellungen des Empfängers dieses Briefes – Urbans II. – vollständig in Einklang stehen würden.'

55 Althoff, *Päpste und Gewalt im Hochmittelalter*, p. 138.
56 G. Strack, 'Pope Urban II and Jerusalem: A Re-examination of his Letters on the First Crusade', *Journal of Religious History, Literature and Culture*, 2 (2016), 51–70.
57 Kb, p. 105.
58 See Strack, 'Urban II and Jerusalem'.
59 Kb, p. 174; trans. *Letters*, pp. 36–7.

FEAR, FORTITUDE AND MASCULINITY IN WILLIAM OF MALMESBURY'S RETELLING OF THE FIRST CRUSADE AND THE ESTABLISHMENT OF THE LATIN EAST[1]

Stephen J. Spencer

In 2011, Kirsten Fenton convincingly argued that the Benedictine monk and author William of Malmesbury defined the First Crusade (1095-9) as a 'Christian masculine space' in Book 4 of his *Gesta regum Anglorum*, composed between 1118 and c. 1125-6.[2] This conclusion was based on two main observations. First, through the distribution of the Latin term *virtus*, William emphasised the crusaders' masculinity, and simultaneously differentiated between the virile Latins and the cowardly Turks.[3] Second, the uniformly antagonistic portrayal of women, both Turkish and Christian, revealed that William attached greater importance to gender distinctions than ethnic divisions, at least regarding the dangers posed by female sexuality.[4]

It will be argued here that this preoccupation with masculinity, and specifically William's intention of pitching the First Crusade as a model of male fortitude for future generations, had a far greater impact on his presentation of events in *Outremer* than has yet been acknowledged. The use of gendered language in Book 4 of the *Gesta regum* will be considered first, before exploring two ways in which this concern for gender shaped William's portrayal of events in the East: namely, the paucity of references to both deserters and instances of Latin fear. The article ends with a comparative case study, analysing how William approached his principal source for King Baldwin I of Jerusalem's career to determine whether his omission of Latin fear was a deliberate narrative strategy. In so doing, this article seeks to advance our understanding of William's account of the First Crusade and the early years of Latin settlement, which remains relatively understudied due to his lack of eyewitness credentials, and to contribute to the growing corpus of scholarship on the gendered presentation of crusading in historical narratives.[5]

Creating 'an incentive to deeds of valour'

That William of Malmesbury perceived crusading in gendered terms is suggested, above all, by the constant imputation of *virtus*, as well as other terms deriving from the same stem, to Latin Christian combatants. Medieval chroniclers inherited a complex etymology of *virtus* from the writers of late antiquity, for whom it possessed a dual meaning, designating both virtue – moral excellence – as well as the martial qualities of courage, strength and manliness.[6] The connection between *vir* (man) and *virtus* meant that, for twelfth-century Latin writers like William, *virtus* had strong connotations of ideal masculine behaviour, although recent research has revealed that the term was frequently used to describe the masculine identities of lay and religious men alike.[7] William of Malmesbury used *virtus* in various grammatical forms a total of forty times in his account of the First Crusade and the early years of the Latin East, almost always to communicate the manly courage of Latin protagonists. Significantly, William justified the incorporation of a history of the First Crusade into Book 4 of the *Gesta regum* by remarking that 'to hear of such a famous enterprise in our own time is worthwhile in itself and an incentive to deeds of valour (*uirtutis*)'.[8] The inclusion of this disclaimer was by no means unique. Fulcher of Chartres, whose *Historia Hierosolymitana* William consulted, clearly appreciated the didactic value of the First Crusaders' actions, announcing in his prologue:

> It is truly pleasing to the living, and also profitable to the dead, when the deeds of brave men, especially of those fighting for God, are either read from writing or, preserved in the recess of the mind, are soberly recited from memory among the faithful.[9]

Nor did William of Malmesbury necessarily conceive of the crusaders' actions as the only deeds of valour worthy of remembrance and imitation. In the prologue to his final historical work, the *Historia Novella*, William remarked: 'Further, what is more pleasant than consigning to historical record the deeds of brave men, so that following their example the others may cast off cowardice and arm themselves to defend their country?'[10] Yet this narrative agenda of presenting acts of manly prowess as exemplars for future generations appears to have been especially influential in conditioning William's treatment of the First Crusade and events in *Outremer*. Indeed, for William, even the valiant heroes of antiquity were inadequate comparators, since they fought for worldly splendour rather than God. As such, he maintained that the virile deeds performed by the First Crusaders surpassed those of the ancients and should be prioritised accordingly:

> Nothing to be compared with their glory has ever been begotten by any age. Such valour as the ancients had vanished after their death into dust and ashes into the grave, for it was spent on the mirage of worldly splendour rather than on the solid aim of some good purpose; while of these brave heroes of ours, men will enjoy the benefit and tell the proud story, as long as the round world endures and the holy Church of Christ flourishes.[11]

The same idea, that the First Crusaders transcended the ancients as role models, can likewise be discerned in William's description of the Latins' lachrymose worshipping at the Holy Sepulchre on 15 July 1099, in which he suggested that even the ancients, such as Orpheus, would be unable to number the tears poured forth to God that day.[12]

The First Crusaders' virility was firmly established in William's account of Urban II's Clermont sermon, in which the pope juxtaposed the Christians' manful courage with the timidity of the Turks, who fought with *virus* (venom) rather than *virtus*. They were thus deemed 'the weakest of men' (*homines inertissimi*) – a characteristic determined by climate.[13] The westerners' more temperate climate meant that they possessed the *virtus* that the Turks lacked: 'Go forth', Urban reportedly announced, 'and lay these cowardly nations low! Let the celebrated *uirtus* of the Franks . . . advance.'[14] With the crusaders' manliness established, the remainder of the narrative is peppered with references to their virile courage, appearing primarily in relation to the expedition's leaders. Thus, Godfrey of Bouillon was considered a 'paragon of courage' (*uirtutis specimen*) and his *virtus* was said to have contributed to his selection as Jerusalem's ruler.[15] As has been acknowledged elsewhere, the final portion of William's account was dedicated to the heroic exploits of princes like Bohemond of Taranto, who was 'second to none in courage'.[16]

The Treatment of Deserters

On the basis of the foregoing analysis, we can plausibly postulate that the depiction of the expedition's participants – especially its leaders

– as exemplars of manly valour probably represents a conscious authorial ploy. Yet this appears to have had a significant bearing on several other aspects of the narrative. Remarkably little attention was afforded to those who abandoned the enterprise, despite the fact that William's sources, such as Fulcher of Chartres's *Historia* and the anonymous *Gesta Francorum et aliorum Hierosolimitanorum*, were littered with such stories.[17] There was only a nod towards Stephen of Blois's flight from Antioch in June 1098 and the shame incurred: 'Then it was that Stephen, count of Blois, fled secretly, using lies to turn back new arrivals; and without doubt it is a great reproach to the man, that on the day after his departure the city agreed to surrender.'[18] The various accounts of Stephen's desertion, many of which were based on the *Gesta Francorum*, have already received a great deal of scholarly attention, most recently from Conor Kostick and William Aird, although it is worth noting here that William of Malmesbury's version is significantly shorter than most other accounts of this episode.[19]

William's decision to brush over the count's departure was probably a by-product of political considerations: the *Gesta regum* was originally commissioned by Matilda II, wife of King Henry I, to whom Stephen was related through his marriage to Adela of Blois. Tellingly, this passage was excised from a slightly later version of the *Gesta regum*, perhaps in reaction to the accession of Stephen of Blois's son and namesake to the English throne.[20] However, two additional factors could also explain William's brevity. Fulcher of Chartres only alluded to Stephen's flight in passing, and this event may have conflicted with William's authorial aim of presenting the expedition as an exemplar of masculine behaviour.[21] Such an interpretation is supported by two further references to the expedition's deserters, the first of which represents a more hostile rendering of Fulcher of Chartres's account of Hugh of Vermandois's departure and suggests that William held deserters beyond Stephen in low esteem. After recording the death of Bishop Adhémar of Le Puy on 1 August 1098, Fulcher stated: 'and then Hugh the Great, with the goodwill of the princes, departed for Constantinople, and from there to France.'[22] William, whose description of this episode likewise immediately follows the bishop's passing, made several subtle revisions to Fulcher's account. He omitted the reference to Constantinople (and thus the pretext for Hugh's departure, implied by Fulcher and directly stated in the *Gesta Francorum*, that he was sent to liaise with the Byzantine emperor), cast doubt on the leaders' consent through the addition of 'ut aiunt' (so they say) and seemingly questioned Hugh's motives by having him claim illness: 'and Hugh the Great, with the agreement of the heroes, so they say, returned to France, alleging the incessant contortion of his bowels'.[23] William's final allusion to deserters, which appears in connection to the so-called 1101 Crusade, lays bare his narrative agenda. Detailing the participation of Stephen of Blois, Stephen of Burgundy, Hugh of Lusignan, and Hugh of Vermandois, William wrote that they were 'eager to make good the disgrace of their former withdrawal by some fresh act of deliberate valour (*uirtute*)'.[24] The decision to acknowledge reticent crusaders here can be explained by the fact that their redemption through the 1101 enterprise conformed with, rather than opposed, William's vision of events in the East as a model of manful prowess for readers to emulate.

The Omission of Latin Fear

This consideration seemingly encroached on William of Malmesbury's retelling of the First Crusade in another significant way. One of the striking features of his account is the almost complete absence of crusader fear. Whereas other writers, including the anonymous author of the *Gesta Francorum* and Fulcher of Chartres, recognised moments when Latin combatants experienced terror – even if, for the most part, they considered it an inappropriate emotion – William did so very rarely.[25] This cannot simply be explained by a lack of interest in the emotional experience of crusading, for William purported to 'recount the journey to Jerusalem, reporting in my own words what other men saw and felt'; accordingly, a variety of passions were attributed to participants throughout his account.[26] For example, episodes of Latin joy – usually related using *laetitia* and *gaudium* – punctuate the crusading segment, with William writing of the ability of the sign of the cross to stimulate joy and alleviate toil; the happiness associated with seeing the Holy Sepulchre or receiving the martyr's crown; the glee of those who departed and the sorrow of those left behind; the cheerful shouts which accompanied the war-cry 'Deus uult! Deus uult!'; and the crusaders' delight at the sight of the emir of Antioch's decapitated head.[27] There are no indications that this emotion possessed significant gendered implications for William, although his description of the crusaders expressing the 'joy of their hearts' (*animorum laetitia*) through combat during the siege of Jerusalem, coupled with the frequent imputation of this passion to Latin protagonists, suggests that it was not considered detrimental to their masculine identities.[28]

The remainder of this article therefore offers several feasible explanations for the omission of crusader fear. While William of Malmesbury is renowned for being steeped in classical tradition, this does not appear to have impacted directly on his appraisal of fear, even though he had Urban II recite Lucan: 'no greater are the labour and fear you seek, but higher the reward'.[29] Hagiographical literature probably exercised a more formative influence over William's conception of fear. On the whole, admissions of *timor mortis*, the fear of death, were rare in accounts of saints' lives, including those by William himself.[30] In fact, there is a strong correlation between William's representation of fear in Book 4 of his *Gesta regum* and in his hagiographies, such as the *Vita Dunstani* and *Vita Wulfstani*. In all these texts, faith – or, more precisely, humble trust in God – was the antidote to a terror-stricken mind. Thus, William praised those who settled in the East following Jerusalem's capture in 1099, for they willingly endured 'fear of barbarian attacks' and set 'a memorable example of faith in God'.[31] The sight of demons passing before his eyes did not cause St Dunstan to 'flee in helpless fear', and when the Devil attempted to interrupt St Wulfstan's prayer, the latter repelled his adversary by reciting Psalm 117:6: 'The Lord is my helper; I will not fear what man can do unto me'.[32] Moreover, Wulfstan reportedly reassured mourners at his deathbed that 'none of those you fear will be able to harm you, if you are willing to faithfully serve God'.[33]

Despite Rodney Thomson's conclusion that this chronicler's 'explicitly Christian sentiments in relation to the Crusade are remarkably scarce and very diluted indeed', William's vision of crusader spirituality, and the conceptual link he drew between fearlessness and martyrdom, may also account for the relative absence of fear.[34] While it is unlikely that Urban II had promised the martyr's crown to those who died during the enterprise, the incompatibility of fearing death with the reward of martyrdom was an integral aspect of the pope's Clermont address in the *Gesta regum*. In this, Urban explicitly referred to the reward of 'blessed martyrdom' (*felicis martirii*), before asking his audience:

> Do you fear death, bravest men, outstanding in boldness and courage? Surely nothing human wickedness will be able to devise for you can outweigh heavenly glory; *for the sufferings of this time are not worthy to be compared with the glory that shall be revealed in us*

(Romans 8:18). Can it be, you do not know that, for men, to live is loss [and] to die is happiness?[35]

In light of this reward, the pope continued, 'Why, then, do you fear death, you who love the respite of sleep, which is the image of death? It is without doubt a thing of madness to refuse everlasting life for oneself on behalf of a desire for this short life.'[36] Overcoming the fear of death by meditating on the acquisition of the martyr's crown was, therefore, a central theme of William's version of the pope's exhortation, which suggests a greater interest in crusading spirituality than Thomson appreciated.

While the association between fearlessness and martyrdom was current in just one participant narrative of the First Crusade – Raymond of Aguilers's *Historia Francorum qui ceperunt Iherusalem* – it became markedly more pronounced in several non-participant Benedictine accounts of the early twelfth century.[37] Robert the Monk, Guibert of Nogent and Gilo of Paris all adopted a similar approach to *timor mortis*, recording that the crusaders undauntedly approached death to attain the martyr's crown and denouncing those who failed to do so.[38] For instance, Robert the Monk criticised one fearful warrior (*meticulosus miles*) whose trepidation prevented him from undergoing martyrdom, and the same author later had the crusaders defiantly declare to visiting Fatimid envoys: 'There is no human strength which can instil terror in us at all; because when we die we are born, when we lose temporal life we gain everlasting life.'[39] I would suggest that this shared interpretation of the fear of death – which centred on the ideal of imitating Christ and the reward of martyrdom – is indicative of a common 'emotional community', an interpretative framework proposed by Barbara Rosenwein: 'emotional communities' are 'groups in which people adhere to the same norms of emotional expression and value – or devalue – the same or related emotions'.[40] Admittedly, not all Benedictine chroniclers of the First Crusade engaged with this theme; Baldric of Bourgueil, for one, rarely did so.[41] Nevertheless, on the whole, the relationship between fear and martyrdom was particularly prevalent among early twelfth-century Benedictine commentators, and William of Malmesbury, as part of the same Benedictine 'emotional community', was probably conforming to that rhetorical tradition.

This, in addition to hagiographical conventions, probably helped to shape William's conception of fear, yet I would argue that his preoccupation with masculinity, and especially his presentation of *Outremer* as a place where manly ideals and endeavours were played out, was an even greater contributing factor. Of course, the notion that fear was contrary to the ideal of manhood was not unique to the *Gesta regum*; scholars have long recognised that fear was considered a feminine characteristic in western Europe, and this was reflected in an array of crusade texts.[42] What *is* distinctive about William of Malmesbury's account, however, is the extent to which gendered considerations appear to have directed his attitude to fear. In short, fear was incompatible with the male space that William sought to construct.

An Intrepid King: Baldwin I of Jerusalem

There are several moments when this gender-centred appraisal of fear comes to the fore in the *Gesta regum*, but by far the most revealing section is the 'brief and entirely trustworthy' account of King Baldwin I of Jerusalem's career.[43] For this, William explicitly stated that he was 'placing entire confidence in the words of Fulcher of Chartres, who, [as] his chaplain, wrote a fair amount about him, in a style not indeed rustic but . . . without polish and practice'.[44] Fulcher himself claimed to have written 'in a rustic yet truthful style'.[45] But William did more than simply improve Fulcher's style; he tailored and manipulated his source to suit his narrative agenda.[46] From the outset, Baldwin's crusade participation stemmed from his search for 'splendid opportunities in which [his] *uirtus* could stand out' – something not suggested by Fulcher.[47] The latter's account of Baldwin's subjugation of Tarsus 'with great daring' (*ausu magno*) clearly appealed to William, although, unlike Fulcher, he conveniently ignored the fact that it was seized from a fellow crusader, Tancred of Hauteville, and instead recorded that the citizens willingly accepted him as their lord.[48]

Furthermore, compare their accounts of Baldwin's journey to Edessa in 1097, at the invitation of the city's Armenian ruler, Thoros. Fulcher wrote:

> with his tiny army, that is eighty knights, [Baldwin] proceeded to cross the Euphrates. Having crossed this, we went on very quickly through the entire night [and], very afraid, passed near fortresses of the Saracens that were left here and there.[49]

No such acknowledgement of trepidation features in William's version. Instead, the journey was transformed into a heroic, if perhaps rash, act:

> Baldwin, with just eighty knights, crossed the Euphrates; it was a remarkable display of either courage or rashness (whichever you prefer to say) to advance unhesitatingly with so small an army between surrounding nations of barbarians, whom another would have held suspect either for their nationality or for their unbelief.[50]

A similar recasting of Fulcher's narrative is discernible in William's treatment of the Battle of Nahr al-Kalb, fought in October 1100 during Baldwin's journey to Jerusalem to succeed his brother Godfrey as ruler. Fulcher recorded that Latin scouts notified Baldwin that a narrow pass near Beirut was blocked by a Turkish army, at which Baldwin drew up his forces into battle order.[51] William developed this scene substantially, unusually recognising the trepidation of the scouts, breathless 'on account of fear' (*pro timore*), who served as a foil for the intrepid Baldwin: 'But Baldwin, who was not far short from being the best soldier who ever lived, feared nothing, and resolutely drew up his battle order.'[52] Fulcher then offered a stark admission of fear, noting that the Christians were instructed to pitch camp closer to the enemy 'lest we seemed timid, as we would if we left the place as if fleeing. We showed one thing, but indeed thought another. We pretended boldness, but we feared death... Indeed, I wished rather to be in either Chartres or Orléans.'[53] Conversely, William failed to mention their dread, and instead pitched the entire affair as a calculated strategic move, whereby Baldwin employed a feigned retreat and even ordered his men to allow the enemy to penetrate their formation. As such, the Latins' terror was nothing more than a simulation: Baldwin arranged his men thus to give 'the suspicion of fear' (*suspitionem metus*); and the Latins merely 'pretended fear' (*metum fixisse*).[54]

According to William of Malmesbury, Baldwin never retreated from the field, 'except at Ramla and at Acre' in 1102 and 1103 respectively.[55] Yet, he maintained, both routs were followed by resounding victories, 'because they sprang more from reckless courage than from fear'.[56] In other words, even *inconsiderata virtus* was preferable to *timor*. Whereas other twelfth-century chroniclers warned that excessive boldness could lead to recklessness, in this section of the *Gesta regum*, a relatively sympathetic attitude towards temerity, at least in the performance of courageous deeds, is discernible; as we have seen, William openly acknowledged that

Baldwin's journey to Edessa in 1097 might be considered rash, but still described it in glowing terms. In Baldwin's endeavours, William found – or rather created – 'a model of valour to the whole world'.[57] Though both the aforementioned retreats had initially incurred shame, the king's ability to rectify these setbacks made 'his astonishing and almost divine *uirtus* an inspiration to his contemporaries, just as it will be the admiration of posterity'.[58] William's manipulation and transformation of the 1102 defeat at Ramla into a celebrated triumph and an exposition of Latin virility is further suggested by the fact that his account stands in marked opposition to those by Fulcher of Chartres and Albert of Aachen, both of whom alluded to Baldwin's panic-stricken flight.[59] William did have the king succumb to a temporary moment of hesitation (*hesitabat*), caught between retreating (which would incur shame) and engaging the enemy (which would result in the death of his men), but his eventual decision to fight was represented as a triumph over *metus*: 'Nevertheless, inborn passion conquered, and now fear was made to turn back.'[60]

In addition to the reshaping of Baldwin's career in Fulcher's account, three further considerations suggest that this downplaying of fear was a deliberate authorial decision. The first concerns William's intended audience. As noted above, the *Gesta regum*'s original patron was Matilda II, and after her death in 1118, William revised the text and dedicated it to her stepson, Earl Robert of Gloucester (1121–47).[61] Therefore, in emphasising virile courage and omitting Latin fear, William was probably tailoring his text to satisfy a courtly audience. This also helps to explain why Baldwin was cast as a model of fearlessness, for William displayed a palpable interest in the behaviour and moral standards of kings elsewhere in the *Gesta regum*.[62] Second, when fear does feature in William's account, it is almost exclusively a Muslim passion.[63] The timid Turks, who 'regarded the courage of the Franks with secret dread', serve as a counterpoint to the virile Latins.[64] Their fright was symptomatic not only of their climate, which made them characteristically effeminate, but also of their erroneous faith. The papal legate, Adhémar of Le Puy, was 'especially feared [by the Turks], because they called him the Christians' pope and the instigator of their wars', and God repeatedly struck the crusaders' adversaries with terror.[65] To give just one representative example, the Turks' three successive days of flight from Dorylaeum in July 1097 'testified that something greater than human fear was upon them'.[66] William's distribution of fear terms is thus an important element in his gendered presentation of crusading, achieved through a juxtaposition of the manly, intrepid Latins and the cowardly, fearful Turks. However, there is a notable exception to this trend. Unlike the author of the *Gesta Francorum* and Fulcher of Chartres, William did not portray Kerborgha, *atabeg* of Mosul, as experiencing a dramatic emotional transformation (from pride to fear) during the Battle of Antioch on 28 June 1098.[67] Rather, he recorded that although the Turks fled in panic, their general held fast, 'mindful of his inborn courage'.[68] William's recognition of Kerbogha's *virtus* and departure from his sources here probably reflects a desire to augment Robert Curthose's crusading exploits: he went on to relate that Robert and two compatriots overthrew the virile Kerbogha, the latter having unwisely measured the duke by his small stature alone.[69] However, given William's overarching concern for kingship, this passage can also be read as a commentary on rulership – the message being that even Muslim rulers stood firm in battle.

Finally, there are signs that William perceived other emotions in gendered terms. He rarely depicted the crusaders as weeping, a common marker of emotion in other accounts, with the exception of a passing reference to the tears which filled the air during the Battle of Dorylaeum and the aforementioned description of the Christians' tearful outpourings at the Holy Sepulchre.[70] There is at least one inference that, in certain circumstances, tears were unmanly: on his deathbed in 1100, a stoic Godfrey of Bouillon, whose heart, we are told, was as unconquerable in the face of death as in the midst of the sword, 'often kindly rebuked those who stood weeping'.[71] Moreover, Fenton's examination of William's oeuvre revealed that he regarded the restraint of anger as a marker of masculinity in both lay and religious men, and this perhaps explains the relative paucity of 'anger incidents' in his account of the First Crusade.[72] However, William appears to have suspended this assessment when relating the 1099 conquest of Jerusalem, during which 'the insatiable anger of the victors was devouring'.[73] The crusaders' wrath was characteristically *insatiabilis*, allegedly resulting in the slaughter of 10,000 Muslims in the al-Aqsa mosque, yet there is no hint of criticism or accusation of imperfect masculinity.

Conclusion

For William of Malmesbury, the Holy Land represented an arena for the display of martial prowess and *virtus* – an unambiguously male space. This narrative agenda, it is contended, had a greater impression on his treatment of the First Crusade and events in *Outremer* than has hitherto been recognised. It entailed negating the issue of reticent crusaders, whose abandonment of the enterprise was either downplayed, conveniently sidestepped or introduced only to elucidate ideal masculine behaviour, while potentially awkward events – like Baldwin I's defeats at Ramla and Acre – were transformed into edifying tales of male fortitude. In William of Malmesbury's retelling of the First Crusade and the establishment of the Latin East, we find a story of manly courage, one which had little room for fear. William's reluctance to impute fear to Latin protagonists may be symptomatic of hagiographical conventions and his Benedictine 'emotional community', yet it is also indicative of the degree to which he perceived crusading through a gendered lens. His reworking of Fulcher of Chartres's narrative of Baldwin I's reign, his intended aristocratic audience, his frequent acknowledgement of Muslim terror, and his gendered presentation of other passions all point to the deliberate suppression of episodes of Latin fear – in all likelihood because they conflicted with his broader goal of creating a narrative of virile deeds worthy of emulation. In this respect, William of Malmesbury's text can be legitimately considered as a precursor to the denial of male fear which characterised chivalric literature of the later Middle Ages.[74]

Notes

[1] I am grateful to the editors and Joanna Phillips, who kindly commented on earlier drafts and offered helpful suggestions for improvement.

[2] K. A. Fenton, 'Gendering the First Crusade in William of Malmesbury's *Gesta Regum Anglorum*', in C. Beattie and K. A. Fenton (eds), *Intersections of Gender, Religion and Ethnicity in the Middle Ages* (Basingstoke, 2011), pp. 125–39 (here p. 134). On William's use of gendered language more broadly, see K. A. Fenton, *Gender, Nation and Conquest in the Works of William of Malmesbury* (Woodbridge, 2008), pp. 26–85; K. A. Fenton, 'Men and Masculinities in William of Malmesbury's Presentation of the Anglo-Norman Court', *Haskins Society Journal*, 23 (2014), 115–24.

[3] Fenton, 'Gendering the First Crusade', pp. 128–31.

[4] Fenton, 'Gendering the First Crusade', pp. 131–4.

[5] A. Grabois, 'The Description of Jerusalem by William of Malmesbury: A Mirror of the Holy Land's Presence in the Anglo-Norman Mind', *Anglo-Norman Studies*, 13 (1990), 145–56; R. M. Thomson, 'William of Malmesbury, Historian of Crusade', *Reading Medieval Studies*, 23 (1997), 121–34, revised in R. M. Thomson, *William of Malmesbury*, 2nd edn (Woodbridge, 2003), pp. 178–88; J. Phillips, 'William of Malmesbury: medical historian of the crusades', in R. M. Thomson, E. Dolmans and E. A. Winkler (eds), *Discovering*

William of Malmesbury (Woodbridge, 2017), pp. 129–38; S. B. Edgington and S. Lambert (eds), *Gendering the Crusades* (Cardiff, 2001); A. Holt, 'Between warrior and priest: the creation of a new masculine identity during the crusades', in J. Thibodeaux (ed.), *Negotiating Clerical Identities: Priests, Monks and Masculinity in the Middle Ages* (Basingstoke, 2010), pp. 185–203; M. Mesley, 'Episcopal authority and gender in the narratives of the First Crusade', in P. H. Cullum and K. J. Lewis (eds), *Religious Men and Masculine Identity in the Middle Ages* (Woodbridge, 2013), pp. 94–111; N. R. Hodgson, 'Normans and competing masculinities on crusade', in K. Hurlock and P. Oldfield (eds), *Crusading and Pilgrimage in the Norman World* (Woodbridge, 2015), pp. 195–214; N. R. Hodgson, K. J. Lewis and M. M. Mesley (eds), *Crusading and Masculinities* (Abingdon, 2019).

[6] M. Kuefler, *The Manly Eunuch: Masculinity, Gender Ambiguity, and Christian Ideology in Late Antiquity* (Chicago, 2001), pp. 20, 31, 207–9.

[7] Fenton, *Gender, Nation and Conquest*, pp. 43–55.

[8] WM, vol. 1, p. 542: 'quia tam famosam his diebus expeditionem audire sit operae pretium et uirtutis incitamentum'. All references are to vol. 1, unless otherwise stated.

[9] FC, p. 115: 'Placet equidem vivis, prodest etiam mortuis, cum gesta virorum fortium, praesertim Deo militantium, vel scripta leguntur vel in mentis armariolo memoriter retenta inter fideles sobrie recitantur.' For the redaction used by William, see FC, pp. 82–3; Thomson, *William of Malmesbury*, p. 179.

[10] William of Malmesbury, *Historia Novella*, ed. E. King, trans. K. R. Potter (Oxford, 1998), p. 2: 'Quid porro iocundius quam fortium facta uirorum monimentis tradere litterarum, quorum exemplo ceteri exuant ignauiam, et ad defendendam armentur patriam?'

[11] WM, p. 654: 'Nichil umquam horum laudi comparabile ulla genuere secula; nam et si qua illorum fuit uirtus, in sepulchrales fauillas post mortem euanuit, quod potius in mundialis pompae fumum quam in ullius boni solidum effusa fuerit. Istorum autem fortitudinis sentietur utilitas et ostendetur dignitas quam diu orbis uolubilitas et sancta uigebit Christianitas.'

[12] WM, p. 650.

[13] WM, pp. 600–2. See also pp. 632, 652, 666; Phillips, 'William of Malmesbury', pp. 133–4.

[14] WM, p. 602: 'Ite, et prosternite ignauas gentes! Eat famosa Francorum uirtus.'

[15] WM, p. 658.

[16] WM, p. 692: 'uirtute nulli secundus'. See also Thomson, *William of Malmesbury*, pp. 186–7.

[17] William relied on Fulcher's history and only used the *Gesta Francorum* sporadically: Thomson, *William of Malmesbury*, pp. 179–81.

[18] WM, p. 634: 'Tunc et Stephanus comes Blesensis clam effugit, mendatiis suis aduentantes retro agens, et magno proculdubio hominis improperio, quod sequenti statim die discessionis eius ciuitas deditioni consensit.'

[19] C. Kostick, 'Courage and Cowardice on the First Crusade, 1096–1099', *War in History*, 20 (2013), 32–49; W. M. Aird, '"Many others, whose names I do not know, fled with them": Norman courage and cowardice on the First Crusade', in Hurlock and Oldfield (eds), *Crusading and Pilgrimage in the Norman World*, pp. 13–30.

[20] WM, vol. 2, pp. 318–19.

[21] FC, p. 228.

[22] FC, p. 258: 'et tunc Hugo Magnus Constantinopolim favore procerum abiit, deinde Franciam'.

[23] WM, p. 638: 'et Hugo Magnus, concessu ut aiunt heroum, Frantiam rediit, causatus continuam uiscerum tortionem'; GF, p. 72. For differing accounts of Hugh's infirmity, see J. Phillips, 'Crusader masculinities in bodily crises: incapacity and the crusader leader,

1095–1274', in Hodgson, Lewis and Mesley (eds), *Crusading and Masculinities*, pp. 149–64 (here pp. 157–8).

24 WM, pp. 680–2: 'antiquae discessionis improperium noua et excogitata uirtute sarcire cupientes'.

25 GF, pp. 35, 56, 57, 60, 61, 62–3, 67, 79, 88, 90; FC, pp. 171, 195–6, 211, 222, 228, 244, 246–7, 330; WM, pp. 628, 664, 668.

26 WM, p. 592: 'Nunc iter Ierosolimitanum scripto expediam, aliorum uisa et sensa meis uerbis allegans.'

27 WM, pp. 602, 604, 606, 608, 636. See also the discussion of William's lexicon for pleasure and applause in M. Winterbottom, 'Words, words, words . . .', in Thomson, Dolmans and Winkler (eds), *Discovering William of Malmesbury*, pp. 203–18 (here pp. 212–13).

28 WM, p. 648.

29 WM, pp. 598–600; Lucan, *De bello civili*, ed. and trans. J. D. Duff, The Loeb Classical Library (Cambridge, MA, 1962), 1.182: 'Par labor atque metus, pretio meliore petuntur.' For William's knowledge and use of classical literature, see especially J. Blacker, *The Faces of Time: Portrayal of the Past in Old French and Latin Historical Narratives of the Anglo-Norman Regnum* (Austin, TX, 1994), pp. 58–66; J. G. Haahr, 'William of Malmesbury's Roman models: Suetonius and Lucan', in A. S. Bernardo and S. Levin (eds), *The Classics in the Middle Ages: Papers of the Twentieth Annual Conference of the Center for Medieval and Early Renaissance Studies* (Binghamton, NY, 1990), pp. 165–73; Thomson, *William of Malmesbury*, pp. 48–62; S. O. Sønnesyn, *William of Malmesbury and the Ethics of History* (Woodbridge, 2012), pp. 21–41.

30 V. Fumagalli, *Landscapes of Fear: Perceptions of Nature and the City in the Middle Ages*, trans. S. Mitchell (Cambridge, 1994), p. 26.

31 WM, p. 654: 'metum barbaricorum incursuum . . . memorabili fidutiae Dei exemplo'.

32 William of Malmesbury, *Saints' Lives*, ed. and trans. M. Winterbottom and R. M. Thomson (Oxford, 2002), pp. 232, 28: 'inerti pauore refugit', 'Dominus michi adiutor; non timebo quid fatiat michi homo.' All biblical citations are from the Douay-Rheims version.

33 William of Malmesbury, *Saints' Lives*, ed. and trans. Winterbottom and Thomson, p. 142: 'nec aliquis ex eis quos timetis uobis poterit nocere, si Deo uelitis fideliter seruire.'

34 Thomson, 'William of Malmesbury', 126; Thomson, *William of Malmesbury*, p. 183. See also R. M. Thomson, 'William of Malmesbury's historical vision', in Thomson, Dolmans and Winkler (eds), *Discovering William of Malmesbury*, pp. 165–73 (here p. 168).

35 WM, pp. 602, 604: 'Mortemne timetis, uiri fortissimi, fortitudine et audacia prestantes? Nichil certe in uos poterit comminisci humana nequitia quo superna pensetur gloria; *non enim sunt condignae passiones huius temporis ad futuram gloriam quae reuelabitur in nobis*. An nescitis quod uiuere hominibus est calamitas, mori felicitas?'

36 WM, p. 604: 'Cur ergo mortem timetis, qui somni requiem, quae instar mortis est, diligitis? Res est nimirum dementiae pro cupiditate breuis uitae inuidere sibi perpetuam.'

37 RA, pp. 113–14.

38 For example, see GN, pp. 156, 179; GP, pp. 68–70, 172. I have discussed this uniformity elsewhere: S. J. Spencer, 'The Emotional Rhetoric of Crusader Spirituality in the Narratives of the First Crusade', *Nottingham Medieval Studies*, 58 (2014), 57–86 (here 69–72); S. J. Spencer, 'Constructing the crusader: emotional language in the narratives of the First Crusade', in S. B. Edgington and L. García-Guijarro (eds), *Jerusalem the Golden: The Origins and Impact of the First Crusade* (Turnhout, 2014), pp. 173–89 (here pp. 178–9).

39 RM, pp. 10–11, 48: 'Nulla virtus est humana, que nobis omnino terrorem incutiat; quia cum morimur, nascimur, cum vitam amittimus temporalem, recuperamus sempiternam.'

40 B. H. Rosenwein, *Emotional Communities in the Early Middle Ages* (Ithaca, NY, 2006), p. 2.
41 BB.
42 See the introduction to A. Scott and C. Kosso (eds), *Fear and its Representations in the Middle Ages and Renaissance* (Turnhout, 2002), p. xxv; and for examples, see BB, pp. 31, 66; RC, p. 698.
43 WM, p. 660.
44 WM, p. 660: 'integra et breui ueritate ... fidei soliditate accommodata dictis Fulcherii Carnotensis; qui, capellanus ipsius, aliquanta de ipso scripsit, stilo non quidem agresti sed ... sine nitore ac palestra'.
45 FC, p. 116: 'stilo rusticano, tamen veraci'.
46 On William's use of Fulcher's *Historia* for several episodes (but not Baldwin I's career), see J. O. Ward, 'Some principles of rhetorical historiography in the twelfth century', in E. Breisach (ed.), *Classical Rhetoric and Medieval Historiography* (Kalamazoo, MI, 1985), pp. 103–65 (here pp. 121, 122, 131–2, 144); Thomson, *William of Malmesbury*, pp. 180–2.
47 WM, p. 660: 'splendidas occasiones aucupari quibus uirtus enitescere posset'.
48 FC, pp. 207–8; WM, p. 660.
49 FC, pp. 210–11: 'cum minimo exercitulo suo, scilicet LXXX militibus, pergens transiit Euphratem. Quo transito, nocte tota properpere prope Saracenorum castra, hinc et inde linquentes ea, valde pavidi perreximus'.
50 WM, p. 662: 'Ita Balduinus ... cum octoginta solum militibus Eufratem transmeauit, spectaculo mirando seu dicere uelis fortitudinis seu temeritatis, ut inter circumfusas barbarorum nationes, quas alter haberet uel pro gente uel pro incredulitate suspectas, cum tantillo exercitu non hesitaret procedere'.
51 FC, pp. 357–9.
52 WM, p. 668: 'At Balduinus, qui parum ab optimo qui umquam fuerit milite distaret, nichil perterritus atiem dispositam in eos constanter instituit'.
53 FC, p. 360: 'ne videremur quasi timidi, si locum ceu refuge linqueremus. Sed aliud monstravimus, aliud vero cogitavimus. Audaciam finximus, sed mortem metuimus ... Ego quidem vel Carnoti vel Aurelianis mallem esse'.
54 WM, p. 668.
55 On Baldwin's failed siege of Acre in 1103, and the city's eventual conquest in 1104, see S. B. Edgington, 'The capture of Acre, 1104, and the importance of sea power in the conquest of the littoral', in J. France (ed.), *Acre and its Falls: Studies in the History of a Crusader City* (Leiden, 2018), pp. 13–29.
56 WM, p. 680: 'quod magis inconsiderata uirtute quam timore prouenerint'.
57 WM, p. 684: 'omni seculo ... uirtutis spectaculum'.
58 WM, p. 688: 'Quibus laboribus effecit ut ammirabilis et pene diuina uirtus eius fuerit presentibus stimulo, futura posteris miraculo'.
59 FC, pp. 439, 444–5; AA, p. 642. Albert characterised the king as *uite diffisus* ('despairing of life'), a formulaic phrase he often used in conjunction with fear terminology.
60 WM, p. 684: 'Veruntamen uicit calor ingenitus, et terga iam dabat metus'.
61 Blacker, *Faces of Time*, pp. 12–13; Thomson, *William of Malmesbury*, pp. 36–7; Fenton, *Gender, Nation and Conquest*, p. 23.
62 See B. Weiler, 'William of Malmesbury on Kingship', *History*, 90 (2005), 3–22.
63 WM, pp. 640, 648, 672, 676, 678.
64 WM, p. 670: 'tacito metu Francorum fortitudinem suspitientes'.
65 WM, p. 638: 'maxime metuerent, quia illum papam Christianorum et incentorem bellorum dictitarent'.

66 WM, p. 630: 'abiectis arcubus maius aliquid quam humanum timorem continua trium dierum fuga testati sunt'.
67 GF, pp. 51–6, 66–8; FC, p. 254; S. J. Spencer, 'Emotions and the "Other": emotional characterizations of Muslim protagonists in narratives of the crusades (1095–1192)', in S. T. Parsons and L. M. Paterson (eds), *Literature of the Crusades* (Woodbridge, 2018), pp. 41–54 (here p. 52).
68 WM, p. 702: 'genuinae uirtutis memor'.
69 WM, p. 702.
70 WM, pp. 630, 650.
71 WM, pp. 658–60: 'qui lacrimas astantium sepe benignus cohercuerit'.
72 Fenton, *Gender, Nation and Conquest*, pp. 35–43. See also Weiler, 'William of Malmesbury on Kingship', 9–11.
73 WM, p. 650: 'insatiabilis ira uictorum consumebat'.
74 See A. Taylor, 'Chivalric conversation and the denial of male fear', in J. Murray (ed.), *Conflicted Identities and Multiple Masculinities: Men in the Medieval West* (London, 1999), pp. 169–88.

REFOCUSING THE FIRST CRUSADE: AUTHORIAL SELF-FASHIONING AND THE MIRACULOUS IN WILLIAM OF TYRE'S *HISTORIA IEROSOLYMITANA*[1]

Beth C. Spacey

Introduction: A Reputation for Scepticism

Being the only extant narrative produced in the Latin East in the second half of the twelfth century, Archbishop William of Tyre's (*c.* 1130–*c.* 1186) *Historia Ierosolymitana* is of signal importance to the history of *Outremer*.[2] Born in the Latin kingdom of Jerusalem, William later travelled to Europe (the likely birthplace of his parents) to study at Paris, Orléans and Bologna before returning to the East in 1165. Upon his return he soon rose to prominence in the court of King Amalric of Jerusalem, who granted him the archdeaconry of Tyre in 1167. William began work on his *Historia* between 1170 and 1184, a period during which he also acted as tutor to the future King Baldwin IV of Jerusalem, and then became both chancellor of the kingdom (1174) and archbishop of Tyre (1175). His *Historia* is a chronologically arranged *narratio rei gestae* which traces Jerusalem's fortunes from the Sasanian conquest of 614 until 1184, just two years before his own death.[3] Consequently, the text is particularly valuable as an insight into events relating to the twelfth-century Latin kingdom of Jerusalem and the other polities of *Outremer*. It also offers a significant window onto how an inhabitant of Jerusalem in the later part of the twelfth century both remembered and represented the events responsible for the kingdom's foundation: the expedition now known to posterity as the First Crusade.

Importantly, William's treatment – or rather his apparent lack thereof – of the miraculous in his narrative of the First Crusade has drawn a great deal of scholarly attention.[4] According to the nineteenth-century historian Heinrich von Sybel, William demonstrated a praiseworthy aversion to the miraculous and marvellous, contrasting him with 'the pilgrim or the mere ecclesiastic who writes, caring only for ecstatic visions or penitential practices'.[5] To von Sybel, a pupil of the empiricist scholar, Leopold von Ranke, the miraculous was something 'foreign to [William's] sober and well-regulated mind'.[6] A century later, this line of thinking was continued – albeit more generously – by August Krey, who described William's work as 'less credulous than . . . most contemporary chronicles'.[7] For over a century, therefore, William's allegedly limited focus on the miraculous was seen as evidence of a critical mind before its time; a twelfth-century anticipation of an age of reason and enlightenment.

The explosion of the 'Age of Faith' paradigm in the 1980s and 1990s naturally problematises conclusions which point to William as unusually cynical. Susan Reynolds and John Arnold, among others, have demonstrated the ubiquity of doubt and scepticism among medieval Christians.[8] Consequently, in expressing these attributes, William was by no means as unusual as von Sybel or Krey suggested. While more recent treatments of William have allowed room for this, the idea that he was remarkably sceptical of the miraculous has persisted. In what continues to be the most important and detailed study of William's life and work, Peter Edbury and John Rowe observed that William discarded a considerable proportion of the miraculous and marvellous elements found in his sources, and that 'not much that is miraculous or self-evidently fictitious has got through William's grid'.[9]

More recently, Tuomas Lehtonen has situated William's approach to the miraculous within the Latin Christian intellectual landscape, and more specifically within the twelfth-century rise of 'New Platonisms' and natural philosophy. Lehtonen's examination of the explanatory frameworks employed in William's history revealed that he allowed significant scope for human agency alongside, and often at the expense of, other causal factors, like divine punishment in response to sin.[10] Indeed, given William's schooling in twelfth-century Europe, it is not surprising that he would have been influenced by such developments, which constituted a shift away from the Augustinian sacramental worldview and towards a more restricted role for the miraculous.[11]

It is certainly the case that William employed the miraculous relatively sparingly in his text, and that there are instances where scepticism surrounding authenticity is explicitly voiced. However, an examination of the material that does feature in William's work, focusing in this instance on his treatment of the First Crusade, reveals that he was harnessing the narrative capabilities of the miraculous in two ways.[12] First, William deliberately portrayed himself as a careful curator of anecdotal evidence. This is not to say that he was necessarily less inclined to believe in the veracity of the miraculous than his contemporaries, but that by engaging in a process of authorial self-fashioning, one which legitimised the miracles that he did choose to present, he made instances of omission appear more explicit to modern scholars familiar with William's source materials. Second, what is often seen as omission on William's part can in fact be seen to represent the deliberate refocusing of the miraculous of the First Crusade towards the place of his birth and the central subject of his text: Jerusalem. So, rather than seeing William's restrained and self-conscious use of the miraculous as the result of an unusually sceptical mind, it is perhaps more useful to see William as employing the miraculous selectively; not only on account of the increasingly naturalising cosmology of late twelfth-century Latin Christendom, but also because of its importance to his representation of himself and Jerusalem. Nor should William's appreciation of the value of the miraculous as a narrative ingredient be seen as evidence of a cynical author writing for a believing (or similarly disbelieving) audience: the capacity for belief in miraculous phenomena is not undermined by an appreciation of its rhetorical utility.[13]

Cynicism as Authorial Self-Fashioning

Instances of explicit cynicism in William's *Historia* can be seen to constitute a process of authorial self-fashioning, which in turn makes the miraculous and marvellous that William did choose to present appear especially trustworthy. For example, William recounted a story in which Ida of Lorraine, mother of First Crusade participants Godfrey of Bouillon and Baldwin and Eustace of Boulogne, predicted the roles which her three infant sons would have later in their lives.[14] She is described as a holy and religious woman, who made this prediction under the influence of the 'divine spirit' (*spiritu . . . divino*) as if it had been foretold by an oracle.[15] William goes on to mention an associated example – a certain story about a swan – which he judges to fall short on grounds of believability.[16] The allusion here is to the tradition of the

Swan Knight.[17] The story, which became associated with the brothers' maternal dynasty in the middle of the twelfth century, centres around a mysterious knight notable for a spectacular entrance on a boat drawn by a swan.[18] It is interesting that William chose to mention the story at all, when he could have chosen to omit it, and avoid perpetuating the tradition entirely.

It may be that remaining silent was considered more damaging in some instances than the risk of continuing the tradition; better explicitly to criticise a ubiquitous story than to say nothing. Certainly, by making the omission explicit via the narrator's (which the audience is intended to understand as William's own) voice, an image of William as the shrewd compiler, who would in every instance weigh the veracity of his source material, is cultivated. This inherently subversive act against the allegedly prevailing belief in these anecdotes, identified as mundane by William, in turn encourages a sense of trust in his work and promotes an atmosphere which emphasises the miraculous credentials of the anecdotes which William *did* incorporate.[19] William's contemporary, Henry of Huntingdon (d. *c*. 1157), portrayed himself as engaging in a similar process in the opening of the ninth book of his *Historia Anglorum*, in which he stated: 'I do not openly contradict them [i.e. miracles] unless they are obviously frivolous, nor give them constant affirmation unless I observe them to be fully corroborated by well-known proofs and trustworthy persons.'[20] Indeed, there is precedent for the condemnation of tall tales even among William's own sources. Albert of Aachen, for example, condemned at length a popular story in which a woman and her followers believed that a goose had been inspired by the Holy Spirit.[21]

If William was engaging in a broader tradition of explicitly rejecting marvellous stories as a method of authorial self-fashioning, then why has he been portrayed as unusually sceptical by modern historians? The answer to this question lies in part in William's use of his sources for his account of the First Crusade, which occupies eight of the *Historia*'s twenty-three books. William is believed to have drawn material from the narratives of crusade participants Raymond of Aguilers, Fulcher of Chartres, and the anonymous author of the *Gesta Francorum*, as well as non-participants Albert of Aachen and Baldric of Bourgueil – all of which were written between the closing years of the eleventh century and the first decades of the twelfth century.[22] He also made use of oral evidence.[23] It is his selective use of these sources, and especially the omission of stories of the miraculous contained in his extant written sources, that has contributed to the persistent image of William as cynic.

For example, William follows Albert's *Historia* in situating the origins of the First Crusade with Peter the Hermit and not, as is the case in several of his other sources, with Pope Urban II and his sermon at the Council of Clermont in November 1095.[24] Both Albert and William describe how Peter, while on pilgrimage to Jerusalem at some point before 1095, was overcome with sleep one night while praying in the Church of the Holy Sepulchre. As he slept, Peter experienced a vision of Christ in which he was charged with facilitating the cleansing of the holy places and bringing aid to the servants of Christ in the East. Edbury and Rowe commented that William removed much of the miraculous aspect of Albert's version of these events, and instead chose to use the material relating to Peter to highlight the insufficiencies of the Byzantine empire.[25] While William's version is indeed shorter than Albert's, insofar as Christ's speech to Peter is abridged, the miraculous implications of this event are not compromised. For example, both Albert and William describe Peter's experience as a '*uisione*':

> [AA:] With this wonderful revelation, worthy of God, the apparition [*uisione*] withdrew and Peter was roused from sleep.[26]
> [WT:] Peter woke, comforted in the Lord by the vision [*uisione*] which he had seen and made more inclined to obedience, and in response to the divine admonition, he ended his delay and energetically prepared to return.[27]

More neutral terminology was certainly available to William had he sought to err on the side of caution in his representation of Peter's experience.[28] Rather, he transposes the terms Albert uses, and at points even augments the story:

> [AA:] There, since he was exhausted by prayers and vigils, he was overtaken by sleep. And the majesty of the Lord Jesus was shown to him in a vision.[29]
> [WT:] He passed the night in prayers and vigils and, finally overcome by the stress of emotion, lay down upon the pavement and gave way to the sleep that overpowered him, and when deep sleep overcame him, as it is accustomed to do, he saw our Lord Jesus Christ as if he were standing before him.[30]

William's additions to this passage serve to strengthen Peter's credentials as the recipient of a revelatory vision. While Albert explains that Peter fell asleep through exhaustion, William places additional stress on the reason for Peter's exhaustion – the effort of his extended vigil – and the depth of his sleep. It is likely that William emphasised characteristics redolent of ecstatic vision to encourage confidence in the genuine nature of Peter's experience. So, while William's version of Christ's admonition is shorter, the more concerted legitimisation of Peter's experience enhances the story's verisimilitude. His treatment of Peter the Hermit's vision in no way undermines the implications of the event as a genuinely divine stimulus for the First Crusade, a claim which sits comfortably with William's later contention that the First Crusade was 'divinely ordained'.[31]

While William abridged Albert's version of Peter's vision of Christ, there remain several other instances where William did not include the miraculous material of his source texts. William's use of Fulcher of Chartres's history (notably also written in *Outremer*) as a source for miraculous content is particularly selective: he makes no mention of the crosses found imprinted in the flesh of the crusaders who drowned off the coast of Brindisi in March 1097, or of various signs at Antioch, for example.[32] While it is unclear in what form William had access to his sources, a broad pattern of omission and incorporation reveals that he was guided by his narrative agenda, and not necessarily disbelief in veracity.

The Miraculous and the Representation of Jerusalem

As discussed above, William was born, spent the early years of his youth, and returned to pursue his career, in the kingdom of Jerusalem, his history's thematic axis. According to Edbury and Rowe, 'to William, who had been brought up there, it was the centre of the world in more than just a metaphorical sense'.[33] Beyond reflecting a general sense of loyalty to his *patria*, William's *Historia* can also be seen as a response to contemporaneous pressures experienced across a critical period in the Latin East's history. On 15 July 1174, during the period William was writing, the thirteen-year-old son of the recently deceased King Amalric was crowned Baldwin IV. In addition to the insecurities that often accompanied minority rule, Baldwin also had leprosy, a disease which raised significant dynastic and moral questions.[34] Alongside these concerns was the ongoing desperation of the kings of Jerusalem to secure military aid from the rulers of western Christendom to assist in the ongoing conflict against Zangid, and later Ayyubid, forces – William was part of a delegation sent to attend the Third Lateran Council in 1179 with responsibility to request military support.[35] Notably, William made extensive revisions to his draft of the *Historia* upon his return from the council. Edbury and Rowe, as well as Benjamin Kedar, have explored how these changes reflected a desire not only to make the content more interesting for a potential western audience, but also to better inform that audience of Jerusalem's significance within the Church.[36] This, Kedar argues, was in response to dialogue concerning the primacy of Rome over the patriarchate of Jerusalem, despite the latter's status as the site of the Resurrection. These various factors contributed to a concatenation that led William, both before and after his involvement in the Third Lateran Council, to make authorial decisions emphasising the significance of Jerusalem. This extended to his use of the miraculous.

Examination of the miraculous events included in William's account of the First Crusade reveal that he clustered these phenomena around events at Jerusalem in June and July 1099, and that he did this in a way that represents a departure from the weighting of the miraculous in his source texts. By emphasising the divine nature of the crusader conquest of Jerusalem, William was able to underline the achievement of the First Crusade and demonstrate that the inception of Jerusalem's now beleaguered ruling dynasty was orchestrated by God. Crucially, William was establishing Jerusalem as the unparalleled, divinely recognised goal of the First Crusade and, by extension, as the rightful recipient of aid from future expeditions.

Many of the Latin narratives of the First Crusade situated the bulk of their miraculous content in their accounts of the siege of the crusaders inside Antioch by Kerbogha, *atabeg* of Mosul, which lasted from 5 June 1098 until the climactic Battle of Antioch on 28 June. Arguably the most iconic of these miracles concerned an army of celestial knights seen fighting alongside the crusader forces in the final battle.[37] Of William's known sources for the First Crusade, both the *Gesta Francorum* and Baldric of Bourgueil's *Historia Ierosolymitana*, which used the *Gesta Francorum*, discuss the celestial army at Antioch. According to these, at a critical moment in the encounter, a heavenly force riding white horses and bearing white standards descended from a nearby mountain, led by Sts George, Mercurius and Demetrius.[38]

Another of William's sources for the First Crusade, Raymond of Aguilers, situated the celestial knights earlier in the narrative: at the Battle at Dorylaeum on 1 July 1097.[39] Strikingly, William made no mention of the heavenly armies at either Dorylaeum or Antioch. Yet, William clearly accepted the miracle in principle, as later in his own *Historia* a mysterious knight astride a white horse guided the defeated army of King Baldwin III of Jerusalem back to safe territory after an abortive expedition to seize the castle of Bosra in 1147.[40] Notably, another of William's sources, Walter the Chancellor's *Bella Antiochena* (written between 1114–15 and 1119–22), also engaged with the motif. It was through God's influence, the *Bella Antiochena* explains, that the Seljuk forces at the Battle of Tall Danith on 14 September 1115 mistook the banners of the prince of Antioch, Roger of Salerno, for an innumerable force of white-clad knights.[41] William does not incorporate this instance into his account of the 1115 encounter, either.[42]

While William's account of the battle of Antioch does not feature the celestial knights, it does include a brief description of a heavenly rainfall, or more literally 'dew' (*ros*), that refreshed the crusaders and their horses, and the miraculous multiplication of the crusader forces in the eyes of their enemies.[43] Raymond discussed both in his text, while both Baldric and Albert included the miraculous rain at Antioch.[44] Only Baldric, however, identified it as 'dew' (*ros*), as opposed to Albert and Raymond, who described it as 'rain' (*pluuia* and *imber* respectively). William was clearly picking and choosing when it came to the miraculous of his source materials. While it could be argued that the general outline of the miraculous in William's narrative of the First Crusade mirrors Raymond's, the former's discussion of another important miraculous event renders this explanation insufficient.

On 14 June 1098, while the crusaders were themselves besieged within Antioch, a Provençal peasant named Peter Bartholomew unearthed what was believed to be a relic of the Holy Lance used to pierce Christ's side at the crucifixion. The excavation had begun after Peter had told the Provençal leader, Count Raymond IV of Toulouse, and the papal legate, Adhémar of Le Puy, about a series of visions he had experienced since December 1097. In these, the apostle Andrew revealed to him that the lance was buried in the basilica of St Peter in Antioch.[45] William's sources for these events include the most enthusiastic proponent of Peter and the relic, Raymond, and one of the most damning, Fulcher of Chartres.

William's treatment of these events, by contrast, is brief and non-committal, revealing a rigorously selective use of his sources and a withdrawal from Raymond's heavily partisan account on the one hand, and Fulcher's critical stance on the other.[46] He does not recount the visions individually (unlike Raymond, who described several at length), and he concluded by dispassionately describing the affair as 'uncertain' (unlike Fulcher, who stated that the relic was falsified).[47] He is more generous, however, in describing the effect that the relic's discovery had on the besieged crusaders. To them, he conceded, it was a great consolation. Significantly, he used the same term (*consolationem*) to describe both the Holy Lance of Antioch and the relic of the True Cross discovered in the aftermath of the crusader conquest of Jerusalem in July 1099.[48] So, while William did not deny the effect that the Holy Lance's discovery had on its erstwhile supporters, he appeared much more cautious when it came to lending any credence to Peter Bartholomew and his visions.[49]

Besides the celestial army and Peter Bartholomew's visions, other miraculous episodes that were situated at Antioch in William's sources, but were omitted from the *Historia*, include the visions attributed to Stephen of Valence; an earthquake; various signs in the sky; a wind that masked the noise of Bohemond's men entering the city; the miraculous rescue of a knight who had fallen from his horse; and multiple visions experienced by prospective deserters.[50]

In contrast, when he came to discuss the 1099 conquest of Jerusalem, William was much more forgiving in his acceptance of the miraculous episodes contained in his sources, especially the miraculous of Raymond's account, which he appears to have relied on for much of his information. The first illustrative example of this concerns the posthumous career of Adhémar of Le Puy, who died at Antioch in August 1098. Raymond described seven posthumous appearances of the legate, many associated with the Holy Lance and its legitimacy.[51] While William only incorporated one of these instances into his *Historia*, it is significant that he chose one which took place during the siege of Jerusalem and made no mention of the Holy Lance.

According to both Raymond and William, several witnesses reported that they had seen Adhémar on the day the crusaders breached the city walls, almost a year after his death. While Raymond simply noted that many saw him both in Jerusalem itself and leading the charge over the walls, William bolstered this with an appeal to the good character of the witnesses, stating that they were respected and trustworthy individuals.[52]

In an even further departure from his source, William also stated that Adhémar was not the only crusade participant who died during the course of the expedition to have been witnessed visiting the sacred sites of Jerusalem on 15 July 1099. This, William continued, represented 'great proof' of the future resurrection.[53] It was fitting, he concluded, that the miracle that occurred at the resurrection of Christ (namely, that many saints rose bodily and were seen by many in Jerusalem) should recur for the benefit of those deceased faithful upon the cleansing of the holy places.[54] It was also appropriate that those who had so devoted themselves to the risen Christ through their participation in the expedition should similarly be resurrected 'in spirit'.[55] This material, concerning the sightings of dead crusade participants at Jerusalem and reflecting on resurrection, is William's own, and does not occur in any of his known sources. Its inclusion lends narrative cogency to his version of the First Crusade and speaks to contemporary concerns surrounding the spiritual implications of death before the completion of an armed pilgrimage such as this.[56] Indeed, William's desire to create as 'complete' a conclusion as possible for his account of the First Crusade is also evidenced, shortly after his account of Adhémar's posthumous appearance, in his improvisation concerning Peter the Hermit. According to William, Christian residents in the city who recognised Peter from his visit several years before – events which William presents as the origins of the First Crusade – gave thanks to him for accomplishing that which had been asked of him.[57]

A second example of how William prioritised accounts of miracles associated with the conquest of Jerusalem is particularly striking given his aforementioned failure to discuss the celestial knights at Antioch. During his description of the siege of Jerusalem, William detailed how divine power aided the exhausted Christian forces. A mysterious knight was seen on the Mount of Olives, brandishing a glittering shield and indicating that the crusaders should return to the fray, which they successfully did. The description of the 'bright and shining shield' is an insertion by William, who otherwise lifts the episode from Raymond's text. It is possible, given William's sources and his use of the celestial knight motif elsewhere in the *Historia*, that he made this addition to align the phenomenon with the pervasive motif.[58]

While it cannot be said that William included every single instance of the miraculous or marvellous that his sources associated with the siege of Jerusalem, a noticeable cultivation of this sort of material around these events is identifiable, particularly when compared to his treatment of the battle of Antioch.⁵⁹ He even included an account of a notable episode in which two sorceresses allegedly came out onto the walls of the city to bewitch the crusaders' siege engines, only to be unceremoniously squashed by a projectile flung by those same engines.⁶⁰ These anecdotes, thrown into sharp relief by William's apparent reluctance to discuss the miraculous elsewhere, means that the *Historia*'s version of the First Crusade reached a relative crescendo of divine approbation, as communicated through the miraculous, at Jerusalem. William's message is clear: crusading endeavours in the interests of Jerusalem are spiritually meritorious and supported through divine intervention in the form of miracles.

Conclusion

The nineteenth-century characterisation of William as atypically cynical was derived from expressions of scepticism in the *Historia*, and from William's abridgement of extant source materials. However, examination of his work reveals that such instances should be recognised as part of a process of authorial self-fashioning; a technique through which William sought to enhance the verisimilitude of the miracles he did incorporate. This, alongside William's selective use of his sources for the First Crusade when it came to the miraculous, is important especially given William's method of focusing the miraculous – and by extension proofs of divine approbation – on the crusader conquest of Jerusalem. It was from the events of July 1099 that the Latin Christian kingdom of Jerusalem, which sits at the heart of William's *Historia*, would emerge, a kingdom which he sought to establish more firmly in the western European consciousness of the later twelfth century.

Notes

1. I am grateful to Andrew Buck and Carol Sweetenham for their comments on earlier versions of this article. I would also like to acknowledge the Arts and Humanities Research Council for funding the research from which this article is derived.
2. I follow Peter Edbury and John Rowe in referring to William's text as the *Historia Ierosolymitana*. See P. W. Edbury and J. G. Rowe, *William of Tyre, Historian of the Latin East* (Cambridge, 1988), p. 1. For a Latin edition of the text, see WT. For an English translation,

see E. A. Babcock and A. C. Krey, trans., *A History of Deeds Done Beyond the Sea*, 2 vols (New York, 1943).

[3] On William's life and career, see especially R. Hiestand, 'Zum Leben und zur Laufbahn Wilhelms von Tyrus', *Deutsches Archiv für Erforschung des Mittelalters*, 34 (1978), 345–80; Edbury and Rowe, *William of Tyre*, pp. 13–22.

[4] On the miraculous in medieval crusade histories, see B. C. Spacey, *The Miraculous and the Writing of Crusade Narrative* (Woodbridge, forthcoming).

[5] H. von Sybel, *The History and Literature of the Crusades*, ed. and trans. L. D. Gordon (London, 1881), p. 284.

[6] Von Sybel, *History and Literature of the Crusades*, p. 304.

[7] A. C. Krey, 'William of Tyre: The Making of an Historian in the Middle Ages', *Speculum*, 16/2 (1941), 149–66 (here 163).

[8] On medieval scepticism and doubt, see especially J. van Engen, 'The Christian Middle Ages as an Historiographical Problem', *The American Historical Review*, 91/3 (1986), 519–52; S. Reynolds, 'Social Mentalities and the Case of Medieval Scepticism', *Transactions of the Royal Historical Society*, sixth series, 1 (1991), 21–41; J. Arnold, *Belief and Unbelief in Medieval Europe* (London, 2005); J. Arnold, 'The materiality of unbelief in late medieval England', in S. Page (ed.), *The Unorthodox Imagination in Late Medieval Britain* (Manchester, 2010), pp. 65–95; K. Brewer, *Wonder and Scepticism in the Middle Ages* (Abingdon, 2016).

[9] Edbury and Rowe, *William of Tyre*, pp. 52, 57. Andrew Buck will begin a project titled 'Creating Outremer: William of Tyre and the Writing of History in the Latin East' in 2019, which will re-examine the significance of William's *Historia*.

[10] T. M. S. Lehtonen, '"By the help of God, because of our sins, and by chance": William of Tyre explains the crusades', in T. M. S. Lehtonen, K. V. Jensen et al. (eds.), *Medieval History Writing and Crusading Ideology* (Helsinki, 2005), pp. 71–84.

[11] See especially W. Wetherbee, *Platonism and Poetry in the Twelfth Century: The Literary Influence of the School of Chartres* (Princeton, 1972); P. Dronke (ed.), *A History of Twelfth-Century Western Philosophy* (Cambridge, 1988); and M.-D. Chenu, *Nature, Man and Society in the Twelfth Century: Essays on New Theological Perspectives in the Latin Medieval West*, ed. and trans. J. Taylor and L. K. Little (London, 1997), pp. 1–98. On the miraculous and the rise of naturalising explanations in medieval historical writing, see C. Watkins, *History and the Supernatural in Medieval England* (Cambridge, 2007), pp. 23–67.

[12] Focusing on William's representation of the First Crusade allows for the detailed comparison of the *Historia* and William's known source materials, thereby offering a measure (albeit imperfect) for the incorporation and omission of miraculous anecdotes.

[13] On medieval belief as processual and inherently reflexive, see S. Justice, 'Did the Middle Ages Believe in their Miracles?', *Representations*, 103/1 (2008), 1–29.

[14] All three participated in the First Crusade. Godfrey would go on to become the first ruler of the Latin kingdom of Jerusalem (1099–1100), while his younger brother Baldwin became king of Jerusalem on Godfrey's death (1100–18).

[15] WT, p. 427.

[16] WT, p. 427: 'Preterimus denique studiose, licet id verum fuisse plurimorum astruat narratio, cigni fabulam, unde vulgo dicitur sementivam eis fuisse originem, eo quod a vero videatur deficere talis assertio.'

[17] Simon John has discussed William's omission of this story in the context of the use of oral evidence in First Crusade histories; see S. John, 'Historical Truth and the Miraculous Past: The Use of Oral Evidence in Twelfth-Century Latin Historical Writing on the First Crusade', *English Historical Review*, 130/543 (2015), 277. See also S. John, 'Godfrey of

Bouillon and the Swan Knight', in S. John and N. Morton (eds.), *Crusading and Warfare in the Middle Ages: Realities and Representations. Essays in Honour of John France* (Farnham, 2014), pp. 129–42.

18 John, 'Godfrey of Bouillon and the Swan Knight', p. 130.
19 See especially S. Greenblatt, *Renaissance Self-fashioning: From More to Shakespeare* (London, 1980); L. Delbrugge (ed.), *Self-fashioning and Assumptions of Identity in Medieval and Early Modern Iberia* (Leiden, 2015).
20 HH, p. 623.
21 AA, p. 58. This story is also discussed in GN, p. 331.
22 Edbury and Rowe, *William of Tyre*, pp. 45–6. For surveys of the western European sources for the First Crusade, see S. B. Edgington, 'The First Crusade: Reviewing the Evidence', in J. P. Phillips (ed.), *The First Crusade: Origins and Impact* (Manchester, 1997), pp. 19–28; J. P. Phillips, *The Second Crusade: Extending the Frontiers of Christendom* (New Haven, CT, 2007), pp. 17–36. For Latin editions of these texts, see RA; FC; GF; AA; BB.
23 See John, 'Historical Truth', 274–7, 281, 283, 296.
24 Albert's text is especially valuable on account of its independence from the tradition represented by the participant narratives. Rather, Albert appears to have relied on oral testimony for his *Historia*. See Susan Edgington's introduction to her edition and translation of Albert's work, AA, pp. xxi–lx.
25 Edbury and Rowe, *William of Tyre*, p. 47.
26 AA, p. 6: 'Ad hanc itaque miram et dignam Deo reuelationem, subtracta uisione, Petrus somno expergefactus est.' English translation is Edgington's from AA, p. 7.
27 WT, p. 127: 'Expergefactus Petrus et visione quam viderat confortatus in domino, factus ad obediendum proclivior et divinam admonitionem sequutus moras rumpit inpiger, ad redeundum accinctus.'
28 His discussions of the visions of Peter Bartholomew, discussed below, are proof of this. I argue that a varied lexis of visionary experience is evidenced in crusade narratives and that authors had access to sophisticated discourse on the varieties of visionary experience in my forthcoming book, *The Miraculous and the Writing of Crusade Narrative*.
29 AA, p. 6: 'Ubi sicut orationibus et uigiliis fatigatus somno decipitur. Cui in uisu maiestas Domini Iesu oblata est.' English translation is Edgington's from AA, p. 7.
30 WT, p. 127: 'Ubi cum pernoctans orationibus et vigiliis fatigatus esset impendio, labore victus in pavimento decubuit ut somno satisfaceret irruenti, cumque sopor ut solet se infudisset altius, visus est ei dominus noster Iesus Christus quasi coram positus astitisse.'
31 WT, p. 137: 'Videtur vere divinitus procuratum presens unde loquimur negocium, et verbum vere egressum a domino.'
32 FC, pp. 168–70, 224, 244–7.
33 Edbury and Rowe, *William of Tyre*, p. 173.
34 See B. Hamilton, *The Leper King and his Heirs: Baldwin IV and the Crusader Kingdom of Jerusalem* (Cambridge, 2000).
35 Hamilton, *Leper King*, p. 144.
36 Edbury and Rowe, *William of Tyre*, p. 85; B. Z. Kedar, 'Some new light on the composition process of William of Tyre's *Historia*', in S. B. Edgington and H. J. Nicholson (eds), *Deeds Done Beyond the Sea: Essays on William of Tyre, Cyprus and the Military Orders Presented to Peter Edbury* (Farnham, 2014), p. 9.
37 See especially E. Lapina, 'The Maccabees and the Battle of Antioch', in G. Signori (ed.), *Dying for the Faith, Killing for the Faith: Old-Testament Faith-Warriors (1 and 2 Maccabees) in Historical Perspectives* (Leiden, 2012), pp. 147–59; E. Lapina, *Warfare and the Miraculous*

in the Chronicles of the First Crusade (University Park, PA, 2015); C. Sweetenham, 'When the Saints Go Marching In: The Memory of the Miraculous in the Sources for the First Crusade', in L. Ní Chléirigh and N. Hodgson (eds), *Sources for the Crusades: Textual Tradition and Literary Influences* (Abingdon, forthcoming).

38   GF, p. 69. The episode also features in BB, p. 81; GN, p. 240; RM, pp. 76–7; HH, p. 438; OV, vol. 5, pp. 112–14, 154–6; WM, vol. 1, p. 637. On the significance of the motif in the century following the First Crusade see B. C. Spacey, 'The Celestial Knight: Evoking the First Crusade in Odo of Deuil's *De profectione Ludovici VII in orientem* and in the Anonymous *Historia de Expeditione Friderici Imperatoris*', *Essays in Medieval Studies*, 31 (2015), 65–82.

39   RA, pp. 45–6.

40   WT, p. 733: 'Generali ergo decreto decernunt via superiore, quoniam planior et minus periculosa erat, incedere, cumque ducem non haberent qui agmini preiret et locorum, per que transituri erant, haberet periciam, ecce subito cohortes precedens miles quidam ignotus, albi sessor equi ...'

41   Walter the Chancellor, *Galterii Cancellarii Bella Antiochena*, ed. H. Hagenmeyer (Innsbruck, 1896), pp. 73–4.

42   WT, pp. 532–4.

43   WT, pp. 333, 337.

44   RA, pp. 56–7, 82; AA, p. 236; BB, pp. 79–80.

45   On the significance of the events surrounding the discovery of the relic, see especially C. Morris, 'Policy and visions: the case of the Holy Lance at Antioch', in J. Gillingham and J. C. Holt (eds), *War and Government in the Middle Ages. Essays in Honour of J. O. Prestwich* (Woodbridge, 1984), pp. 33–45; J. France, 'Two Types of Vision on the First Crusade: Stephen of Valence and Peter Bartholomew', *Crusades*, 5 (2006), 1–20; T. Asbridge, 'The Holy Lance of Antioch: Power, Devotion and Memory on the First Crusade', *Reading Medieval Studies*, 33 (2007), 3–36; Sweetenham, 'When the Saints Go Marching In'.

46   Morris, 'Policy and Visions'; France, 'Two Types of Vision'.

47   WT, p. 367; RA, pp. 68–72, 75–8, 84–91; FC, pp. 237–8.

48   WT, pp. 424–5. On William of Tyre's portrayal of the relic of the True Cross, see D. Gerish, 'The True Cross and the Kings of Jerusalem', *Haskins Society Journal*, 8 (1996), 147–9.

49   It is interesting that William chose to follow Albert in identifying Peter Bartholomew as a *clericus*, as opposed to the poor peasant as Raymond identifies him. Thomas Asbridge has argued that William did this to validate Adhémar of Le Puy's belief in the relic. Asbridge, 'The Holy Lance of Antioch', 25.

50   RA, pp. 54, 72–4; AA, pp. 278, 314, 366–8; FC, pp. 224, 244–7.

51   C. Kostick, 'The afterlife of Adhémar of Le Puy', in P. Clarke and T. Claydon (eds), *The Church, the Afterlife and the Fate of the Soul*, Studies in Church History, 45 (Woodbridge, 2009), pp. 120–9.

52   WT, pp. 414–15: 'Ea die dominus Ademarus, vir virtutum et inmortalis memorie Podiensis episcopus, qui apud Antiochiam, ut prediximus, vita decesserat, a multis in sancta visus est civitate, ita ut multi viri venerabiles et fide digni eum super civitatis murum primum omnium ascendisse et ceteros animasse ad ingressum oculis corporeis se vidisse constanter assererent ...'

53   WT, p. 415. William reveals something of a preoccupation with resurrection in the *Historia*. Later in the *Historia*, he discusses a conversation between himself and King Amalric, in which the latter asked for proof of the future resurrection. See WT, p. 867. Susan Reynolds has suggested that this anecdote reflects doubt on William's part, Reynolds, 'Social Mentalities', 33.

54 WT, p. 415: '... ut sicut resurgente domino multa corpora sanctorum qui dormierant surrexerunt et in civitate sancta apparuerunt multis, ita fidelibus populis, sanctae resurrectionis locum a gentili supersticione mundantibus, priscum renovaretur miraculum...'
55 WT, p. 415.
56 See J. Riley-Smith, 'Death on the First Crusade', in D. W. Loades (ed.), *The End of Strife* (Edinburgh, 1984), pp. 14–31; J. Flori, 'Mort et martyre des guerriers vers 1100: L'exemple de la première croisade', in *Cahiers de civilisation médiévale*, 34 (1991), 121–39; H. E. J. Cowdrey, 'Martyrdom and the First Crusade,' in P. W. Edbury (ed.), *Crusade and Settlement: Papers Read at the First Conference of the Society for the Study of the Crusades and the Latin East and Presented to R. C. Smail* (Cardiff, 1985), pp. 46–56; M. Tamminen, 'Who Deserves the Crown of Martyrdom? Martyrs in the Crusade Ideology of Jacques de Vitry (1160/70–1240)', in C. Krötzl and K. Mustakallio (eds), *On Old Age: Approaching Death in Antiquity and the Middle Ages* (Turnhout, 2011), pp. 293–313.
57 WT, pp. 415–16.
58 It is especially reminiscent of the 'glittering arms' (*armis coruscis*) of the mysterious knights at Dorylaeum, according to Raymond. Cf. RA, pp. 45–6.
59 For example, Albert describes a vision in which Godfrey was seen to climb a golden ladder to heaven: AA, pp. 436–8.
60 WT, pp. 406–7. Cf. RA, p. 149.

REMEMBERING JERUSALEM: LAMENTING THE HOLY CITY IN OCCITAN LYRIC, c. 1187–c. 1300

Lauren Mulholland

In c.1267, shortly after Louis IX of France (1214–70) took the cross as leader of the Eighth Crusade, an anonymous troubadour composed the lyric *El temps quan vey cazer fuelhas e flors*. Consisting of five stanzas and one *tornada* (a shorter, final stanza common to troubadour lyric), the poem exhorted western leaders to liberate Jerusalem. In the second stanza, the poet urged his listeners to remember and protect the Holy City:

> And in front of us is the mirror that was given equally to all of us, Jerusalem, where Jesus was bound and died on the True Cross, and his body was placed in the true sepulchre; and it would be good not to forget such a precious mirror that will soon be obliterated if we do not take it from the infidels.[1]

The emphasis on the need to remember Jerusalem, and the reference to Christ's Passion are frequent tropes in troubadour depictions of the city following its fall to Saladin in 1187, demonstrating that the memory of Latin control of Jerusalem, and its significance to western Christendom, remained a tangible spectre in Occitan culture even after the Holy City's fall to Muslim rulers.

This article seeks to chart these processes of remembrance. It builds on previous scholarship that has demonstrated how depictions of Christ's Passion were used as a stimulus to remember the Holy City by suggesting that these representations served to establish Jerusalem as a place of lamentation and sorrow, linked both to the biblical past and contemporary events. The article begins by outlining troubadour interaction with the crusading movement and some of the ways in which the crusades were remembered in Occitania. From there, the focus shifts to troubadour responses to the loss of Jerusalem, beginning with lyrics composed in the immediate aftermath of 1187 and then moving to those from the thirteenth century. Particular consideration is given to a lyric by Peire Cardenal (c. 1180–c. 1278), which will be used to consider how ancestral memory, alongside remembrance of the True Cross, may have been used to encourage listeners to support crusading efforts. Furthermore, the article will show that depictions of the Passion became increasingly graphic as the thirteenth century progressed, linked to the rise of affective piety and devotion to Christ's humanity. While many of the lyrics discussed here clearly engage with the crusades, I will also draw on examples of works that contain no direct reference to Jerusalem nor call to take the cross, thereby affording a broader view of memories of the Holy City in troubadour lyric. It will be argued, in sum, that to remember Jerusalem in thirteenth-century Occitania was to grieve for both Christ's Passion there in the biblical past and the city's troubled present.

The Troubadours and the Crusades

While troubadours are perhaps still most frequently associated with the courtly love lyric, their corpus of 2,500 songs by 460 poets dealt with a range of topics, including major contemporary events, particularly, as scholars have noted, the crusading movement.[2] The poets used their lyrics both to praise and criticise the leaders of the crusades, to offer commentary on events in the Holy Land, and to encourage their noble listeners to take the cross. While the extent to which such commentary reflected and shaped the opinions of their audience is an area of much debate, the poets' interaction with the crusading movement offers a valuable insight into Occitan perceptions of, and attitudes towards, both the crusades and the Holy City.[3] An understanding of troubadour representations of Jerusalem is all the more pertinent given that Occitania provided crusade participants and settlers for the newly formed 'crusader' states from their very inception, most famously Count Raymond IV of Toulouse (1041–1105), one of the main leaders of the First Crusade and progenitor of the county of Tripoli.[4] Indeed, thirteenth-century poets sometimes invoked the memory of nobles who had participated in earlier expeditions in order to encourage their successors to emulate their ancestors, often criticising the current generation of western leaders for lacking the bravery of their predecessors.

In the 1230s, for example, the Gascon troubadour Aimeric de Belenoi stated that people were 'losing the conquest gained in the Holy Land by our ancestors'.[5] In *c.* 1222, the troubadour Peirol, returning from a Holy Land pilgrimage, lamented that in King John of England (1166–1216), and perhaps also his son, Henry III (1207–72), England had but 'bad recompense' for Richard I (1157–99).[6]

The role of ancestral memory in shaping noble responses to crusade preaching has been the subject of recent scholarship, with the work of Nicholas Paul of particular relevance to Occitania.[7] Paul examined how the crusades were remembered by twelfth- and thirteenth-century noble families, and how these memories of crusading ancestors influenced their successors. He used the Limousin in Occitania as an example of an area in which the memory of the First Crusade was particularly strong, as demonstrated by the crusade memorabilia displayed there.[8] These memorabilia, along with relics of the True Cross and other items associated with Christ's Passion that were brought to Occitania in the wake of the First Crusade, acted as visual prompts which enabled those in the region to remember the Latin army's victory in the Holy City in July 1099. The conquest of Jerusalem was also commemorated liturgically, and Cecilia Gaposchkin has shown that Masses dedicated to the Latin victory, and more specifically to the Holy Sepulchre, were established in Occitania at the abbeys of Beaulieu, Moissac and possibly also Saint-Michel de Cuxa.[9] However, in the aftermath of Hattin, these liturgical celebrations were replaced by the *Clamor pro terra sancta*, which was introduced in 1188 and used until the sixteenth century.[10] The *Clamor*, which acted as both a lament for the loss of Jerusalem and as a means of encouraging new expeditions to the Holy Land, was practised across a wide geographic area that included England, Germany, northern France, and Occitania.[11] Just as the loss of the Holy City was remembered liturgically, so too was it evoked in troubadour lyric.

Remembering the Loss of Jerusalem and the True Cross

As Linda Paterson's recent study of the crusading lyric has shown, the Battle of Hattin, the Fall of Jerusalem, and the subsequent Third Crusade elicited the largest number of responses from the troubadours and their northern French counterparts, the trouvères.[12] Perhaps unsurprisingly, given the potency of the True Cross as symbol of Christ's sacrifice and the promise of salvation, the troubadours often invoked it as a means of remembering its loss during the kingdom of Jerusalem's defeat at Hattin. In a lyric composed c. November 1187, Bertran de Born (d. 1215), lord of Hautefort in the Périgord, lamented the loss of the True Cross relic and urged his listeners to travel overseas to aid in crusading efforts:

> Our Lord himself calls all those who are spirited and worthy and noble; never before has a war or skirmish distressed him, but by this one he is greatly hurt; for the True Cross and the king are taken, and the Sepulchre is in need of aid.[13]

Composed at approximately the same time as Bertran de Born's lyric, the Toulousain poet, Peire Vidal's (fl. 1183–1204) *Anc no mori per amor ni per al*, also highlighted the importance of taking the cross, with the capture of the True Cross and the Holy Sepulchre presented as key reasons to do so:

> I send my song there, to the celestial king, whom we must all honour and obey, and it is necessary that we go there and serve him there where we shall gain spiritual life; because the Saracens, disloyal Canaanites, have taken his realm and destroyed his people, for they have seized the Cross and the Sepulchre, and because of this we should all have great fear.[14]

As we move into the thirteenth century, the True Cross remains a potent symbol in troubadour lyric, even in those poems that do not directly call on their listeners to travel to Jerusalem. Consider, for example, *Dels quatre caps que a la cros*, composed by Peire Cardenal, a poet from Le Puy-en-Velay. The lyric is a paean to the Cross, which is presented as a salvific object that symbolises Christ's authority. No elements within the lyric allow us to date it accurately, and this uncertainty has implications for our understanding of the poet's presentation of the Holy City. René Lavaud suggested that it was composed c. 1201, shortly after Peire Cardenal abandoned his clerical training in order to return to the secular world. For Lavaud, the work was evidence of 'a young former cleric [who] remained a fervent believer and who used his talent on the pious theme of the Cross'.[15] The most recent editor of Peire Cardenal's work, Sergio Vatteroni, argued that the lyric dates to c. 1215. He based this theory on conceptual and linguistic similarities between *Dels quatre caps que a la cros* and a lyric composed in late July 1215 by the Toulousain poet Guilhem Figueira (*c*. 1195–*c*. 1250), *Totz hom qui ben comens'e ben fenis*, arguing that it was composed shortly after Peire Cardenal's panegyric to the Cross.[16] While Vatteroni's argument is plausible, neither his suggested dating, nor that of Lavaud are conclusive, and at best we can cautiously date the lyric to the first quarter of the thirteenth century.

In the second stanza of the lyric, the poet describes the Cross as the 'true standard of the King on whom all depends'.[17] Previous editors have rightly noted that the representation of the Cross as God's 'flag' or 'standard' is a common religious image, found in the liturgy for the exaltation of the Holy Cross and also in hymns, such as Venantius Fortunatus's (530–609) famous *Vexilla regis prodeunt*, which was used for Mass on Good Friday.[18] However, the True Cross acquired a different meaning after the conquest of Jerusalem in 1099; following the discovery of a fragment of the True Cross in the Church of the Holy Sepulchre, the relic was henceforward carried into battle at the head of the Latin army of the kingdom of Jerusalem.[19] Thus, the depiction of the Cross as the 'standard of the king' may have a double meaning, referring both to the True Cross as symbol of Christ's Passion and of God's power, and its relic as the standard of the kingdom of Jerusalem's army. At the time of the lyric's composition in the early thirteenth century, the relic of the True Cross remained lost following the Battle of Hattin. Megan Cassidy-Welch has recently described the loss of the True Cross as an 'acute ontological disruption', which was remembered throughout the thirteenth century in both textual and artistic depictions of the loss of the relic at Hattin.[20] In evoking the True Cross as the king's standard, Peire Cardenal may thus have been encouraging his listeners to remember events in the recent past. If we consider the lyric's *tornada* then we may further argue that the poet was also urging his listeners to travel to the Holy Land to recover this most precious relic.

The *tornada* promises salvation to anyone who 'takes up the cross and follows Christ wherever he goes'.[21] These lines echo Matthew 16:24, and previous editors disagree as to whether the lyric is a call to listeners literally to take the cross and travel to the Holy Land or simply a hymn to the Cross that encourages its listeners to live according to Christ's teachings. Certainly, it would make sense for the poet to urge his audience to follow Christ's example in order to regain Jerusalem, as the blame for Hattin and the loss of the Holy City was laid not simply on those in the

Holy Land, but rather on the iniquity of all Christian people.[22] However, Lavaud, who classified the lyric as a hymn for the crusade, contended that Peire Cardenal used this lyric to encourage his audience to travel to the Holy Land as part of the Fourth Crusade.[23] If Lavaud's dating of 1201 is accepted, then we might see ancestral memory at work in the lyric. In 1201, Peire Cardenal enjoyed the patronage of Raymond VI of Toulouse (1156–1222) and the poet's likely audience mainly comprised the male nobility who made up the majority of the count's entourage.[24] The noble audience could understand the instruction to 'take up the cross' as a direct call to travel to the Holy Land. In drawing attention to the Cross as banner of both God and the Latin army, Peire Cardenal may have reminded his listeners of the deeds of those who captured Jerusalem. Of particular importance here is the fact that the great-grandfather of Peire Cardenal's patron was the aforementioned hero of the First Crusade, Count Raymond IV of Toulouse.

An appeal to ancestral memory is more problematic if Vatteroni's dating of *c.* 1215 is correct. This situates the lyric during the Albigensian Crusade (1209–29), when Raymond VI was one of the leaders of the Occitan army. Previous scholarship has shown that troubadours composing in Provence and Languedoc at the time of the Albigensian Crusade were fiercely opposed to it, and used their lyrics to criticise the actions of the pope, the clergy and the northern French crusading army.[25] Indeed, Peire Cardenal's lyrics from that time include condemnation of the clergy and secular leaders for having 'forgotten' the Holy Sepulchre and the 'land where Christ was born'.[26] It therefore seems extremely unlikely that he would have used his lyric to encourage support for the Albigensian Crusade. During the crusade, the troubadours often presented the Holy Land as the legitimate theatre of war in an attempt to divert crusading efforts away from Occitania. For example, the Tarascon troubadours, Tomier and Palaizi, described the Albigensian Crusade in *De chanter farai* as a 'false crusade' and the French crusaders as 'false absolved fools'.[27] Peire Cardenal's contemporary, Guilhem Figueira, castigated the Church for doing 'little damage to the Saracens' and instead killing Christians.[28] Perhaps Peire Cardenal's lyric forms part of these attempts to remind listeners of the importance of the Holy Land and dissuade the northern French from participating in the continued crusade in Occitania. If the *c.* 1215 dating is correct, the poem coincides with the preaching of the Fifth Crusade, adding to the possibility that Peire Cardenal was drawing attention to the Holy Land. While such a reading must remain speculative, the poem, even if composed c. 1215, may still be read as a commemoration of the biblical past and recent events, given the remembrance of the loss of the True Cross relic throughout the thirteenth century. The Cross as 'standard' called to mind God's sacrifice and also the ongoing failure of the Latin army to recapture the Holy City.

Yet, while the lyrics cited thus far have emphasised the importance of the Cross and its salvific nature, they have not demonstrated any particular attention to Christ's humanity. We shall now consider how attentiveness to Christ's suffering became a noticeable feature of troubadour lyric and the extent to which devotion to the suffering saviour can be linked to contemplation and remembrance of Jerusalem.

The Suffering Christ and the Plight of the Holy City

In the course of the early twelfth century, attention to Christ's humanity became more evident in theological and devotional writings and, from its monastic origins, this new focus on Christ's humanity – with its increasing attention on his suffering on the Cross – quickly spread beyond the cloister.[29] Thus, twelfth- and thirteenth-century artistic and sculptural depictions of Christ on the Cross became increasingly detailed and graphic, in contrast to earlier representations of the crucified saviour as serene, peaceful and alive.[30] This devotion to Christ's humanity also formed part of the crusading movement, with the desire to act in imitation of Christ a motivation for those who took the Cross, and Christ's Passion on the cross a motif in crusade preaching.[31] Importantly, this change towards emphasis on Christ's suffering and vulnerability was mirrored in Occitan lyric.

That the troubadours interacted creatively with religious teaching and devotional trends is well known. Indeed, previous scholars of the Occitan crusading lyric have noted that the poets engaged with devotion to Christ's humanity, which has been tied to a more sombre tone that emerges in crusading lyric in the thirteenth century. Jaye Puckett, for example, has argued that a distinctly darker, pessimistic tone is found in troubadour crusading poetry from the second decade of the thirteenth century. While this darker tone emphasised the continued failure of Latin armies to reclaim the Holy City, Puckett also contended that it was more closely linked to the launch and development of the

Albigensian Crusade, which, as we have seen, the poets opposed and criticised.[32] Paterson also examined the more sombre and sober tone in lyrics relating to the crusades that were composed following Hattin, linking this to broader shifts in Occitan courtly culture. To reconcile the tension between courtly values and the new religious sensibility following Hattin, which emphasised humility and self-criticism, the poets increasingly presented taking the cross as a way for noblemen to prove their worth by serving God, with representations of Christ's death used as a call to action.[33] In an appendix to Paterson's study, moreover, Marjolaine Raguin-Barthelmebs analysed the rhetoric of the crusading lyric, noting – albeit briefly – that the poets appealed to affective piety.[34] However, while Puckett, Paterson and Raguin-Barthelmebs concentrated solely on lyrics relating to the crusades in their assessment of a darker tone in troubadour composition, it should be noted that attention to Christ's agony on the cross occurs in lyrics that have not been traditionally tied to the crusading movement. By considering lyrics relating to the crusades alongside those that contain no call to take the cross, a more nuanced picture emerges, one that shows how Jerusalem was established and remembered as a place of sorrow in the troubadour corpus. An examination of this broader corpus also demonstrates that memories of the crusades formed only one part of a wider process of lamenting Jerusalem in Occitan lyric and this in turn highlights the importance of not isolating crusading memory from broader social and religious shifts.

In the earliest troubadour lyrics, those of William IX of Aquitaine (1071–1127), Marcabru (fl. 1130–49), Jaufré Rudel (fl. 1125–48), and Cercamon (fl. 1137–49), there are no detailed depictions of Christ's Passion and little attention to his humanity. Rather, it is not until later in the twelfth century that descriptions of the Passion appear. For example, they can be found in the work of Peire d'Alvernhe, a troubadour from Clermont who was active in the second half of the twelfth century. In *Lauzatz sia Hemanuel*, which is based on the Athanasian Creed, the poet outlined events from the Gospel accounts of the Passion, including the trial before Pontius Pilate, the lots cast for Jesus' clothes, and the pardon of the penitent thief. The lyric also described that Christ 'suffered Passion' for humanity's salvation.[35] Similarly, in *Cui bon vers agrada auzir*, composed c. 1170, Peire d'Alvernhe drew on the salvific nature of the crucifixion to encourage his audience to remember Christ's suffering and to live a good Christian life while there was still time:

> Whoever looks directly at the crucifix should well think of death, for God suffered death in order to save us, and the one who was placed on the Cross for us killed death, all will die, and wealth will not save us any more than it did Job.³⁶

Once again in this stanza, and indeed throughout the eight-verse lyric, there is no description of Christ's Passion. The stanza is, however, addressed to those who look at the crucifix, and the troubadour may here be acting as preacher, guiding his listeners in their understanding of Christ's Passion.³⁷ His listeners are instructed to consider not only their own death, and the need to live according to Christ's teaching in order to gain salvation, but also the death that Jesus endured on their behalf.

In the final decade of the twelfth century, Occitan lyric descriptions of the Passion, and in particular the crucifixion, become even more detailed. In *c.* 1190, Bernart de Venzac (fl. 1180–1210), a troubadour from the Rouergue in south-central Occitania, described the crucifixion in the fifth stanza of the religious lyric *Lo Pair'e·l Filh e·l Sant Espirital*:

> He who for us shed his natural blood, and gave himself up, and surrendered himself, and was raised on the Cross, and nailed to it and crowned with thorns, grant that on the day of judgement he does not remember our sins, but rather with great joy may he lead us to his dawn.³⁸

Imploring God to forgive sins on the Day of Judgement, Bernart de Venzac focused on the details of the crucifixion and reminded his listeners of the nails, the crown of thorns, and of Christ no longer simply 'suffering' but shedding 'his natural blood'. These lines demonstrate a shift from the implicit Passion of earlier troubadour lyric, in which Christ's suffering was not detailed, to the thirteenth-century poems that provided increasingly graphic descriptions of the crucifixion.

In a lyric composed *c.* 1213, the Auvergnat troubadour Pons de Capdoill (d. *c.* 1236) described the events of the crucifixion, again with attention to the blood Christ shed for humanity:

> Now we may know what He did for us: for He allowed himself to be crowned with thorns, to be beaten, struck and given gall to drink, and He redeemed us with his precious blood. Alas wretched people! They act so badly, those who do not go there [to the Holy Land] and

here think to remove land unjustly from their neighbours. They will need to have fear on Judgement Day!³⁹

Pons de Capdoill here uses the memory of Christ's suffering to exhort his listeners to take the cross, criticising those who fail to do so. Similar sentiments are found in the work of Falquet de Romans (fl. *c.* 1219–33), who in the late 1220s urged Emperor Frederick II (1220–50) to fulfil his crusading vow by reminding him of Christ's sacrifice on the cross:

> Now I entreat the good emperor who has taken the cross to serve God, to go with force and strength to the land where God wanted to die and put his body as a pledge; He was raised on the Cross for us and every man is damned who sees how He was nailed and beaten and wounded for us and who now has no courage.⁴⁰

This attention to Christ's suffering continued throughout the thirteenth century, for example with Pujol in the 1230s describing how Christ was 'killed with great contempt and was struck so that the blood dripped down', and Raimon Gaucelm de Béziers in the 1260s lamenting that God suffered 'grave torment' and died in 'great agony'.⁴¹ All these examples demonstrate an increased attention to Christ's humanity and suffering during the crucifixion, an emphasis that reflects the broader shift in religious culture towards devotion to his humanity. But how does this heightened perception of Christ's suffering inform us about remembrance of the Holy City? In tandem with attention paid to the details of Christ's suffering during the Passion in the lyric, we also find more frequent depictions of Jerusalem, and the Holy Land more broadly, as the site of the Passion. To give but a few examples: it is the 'place where Jesus Christ was born and lived and was raised on the Cross'; 'the place where we were redeemed', and 'the place where God wept' – this final example referring to Jesus weeping over Jerusalem as described in Luke 19:41.⁴² Importantly, the shift towards contemplation of Christ's suffering in Jerusalem came at a time when events there were the cause of shock, grief and confusion in western Europe. It is undoubted, moreover, that such awareness was particularly keen in areas, like Occitania, which had traditionally and intensively participated in crusading efforts from their inception.

Following the loss of Jerusalem, as the examples above have demonstrated, the Holy City was frequently depicted by the troubadours as a place of suffering and death. While the lyrics most often show attentiveness to remembrance of Christ's agony during the Passion, there is also evidence that the poets considered Christ's suffering to be ongoing as a result of the loss of Jerusalem. Following on from this loss, therefore, the Holy City itself could be viewed as an object of mournful remembrance and contemplation. In a lyric composed in 1188, the Limousin poet, Giraut de Borneil (c. 1138–1215), 'grieve[d]' for the damage done to the Holy Land.[43] In another piece composed at approximately the same time, he lamented the 'hurt and insult' endured by God while noblemen refused to take the cross.[44] This sense of grief was also established in the above-cited lyric of Bernart Alanhan de Narbona that described Jerusalem as the place where 'God wept'. In this lyric, which dates to 1229–44, the poet links God's weeping over Jerusalem with anger at the fact that few people go to 'tearfully kiss the Cross' in the place where Jesus wept.[45] For the poet, remembering the Holy City was not just to grieve for it, but to shed tears for it. This depiction is in line with the devotional trend that emerged, particularly from the late twelfth century onwards, in which tears and weeping were increasingly associated with the expression of piety, even in a crusading context.[46] The poet may thus have intended that the tears shed at the cross would be ones of joy, representing the happiness and hope for salvation felt by those who had travelled to *outramar*. However, given the overall sombre tone of the lyric, with its reference to the 'severe torment' (*greus turmens*, line 11) suffered by Christ and its criticism of the inaction of those in the West, we must allow for the possibility that for Bernart Alanhan de Narbona, as for other Occitan poets, to remember Jerusalem in thirteenth-century Occitania was to grieve for the city.

Conclusion

This article has demonstrated that the memory of Jerusalem functioned in several ways in troubadour lyric following the loss of the city. The True Cross and the Holy Sepulchre were frequently used as a means of reminding listeners of what had been lost in the Holy Land and of the importance of reclaiming Christ's patrimony. From the late twelfth century onwards, Jerusalem's loss was increasingly associated with depictions of Christ's suffering during the Passion, invoked as a means of encouraging listeners to remember both the biblical past and the ongoing plight of the Holy City.

Peire Cardenal's paean to the Cross demonstrated the ambiguity that is characteristic of much troubadour lyric. It is difficult to know whether or not the lyric should be read as a call to take the cross, and if so, whether the poet's depiction of the cross as the 'standard' of the king was a means of using ancestral memory to prick the conscience of a noble audience. While the noblemen among Peire Cardenal's listeners may have heard a literal call to take up their own cross and follow Christ in the Holy Land, for others the lyric suggested a figurative assumption of the cross, requiring them to live according to Christ's precepts. Even just by imitating Christ while remaining in Occitania, the lyric's audience would both guarantee their salvation and, given the papacy's increased emphasis, following Hattin and the loss of Jerusalem, on the role of Christian society in contributing to the success of Latin armies overseas by leading sinless lives, also contribute to the recovery of the Holy Land. It is also evident that the memory of Jerusalem was important to all Christians, as is demonstrated by lyrics that do not relate to the crusades, yet which invoke the Holy City. The poems cited above by Peire d'Alvernhe, Pujol and Bernart de Venzac make no reference to taking the cross, or explicitly to Jerusalem; and yet, whether detailing Christ's agony during the Passion, or instructing their listeners on how to respond to the crucifix, their subject matter is intrinsically linked to the Holy City. As was noted in the anonymous lyric that opened this article, the Holy City was a place given 'equally' to all Christian people and it was only when all remembered Jerusalem and the sacrifice Christ made there, that the city – the 'light of salvation' (*lums de salvamen*, line 9) – would be returned to Latin control.

Notes

[1] Anonymous, *El temps quan vey cazer fuelhas e flors*, ed. A. Sakari, 'La chanson de croisade *El temps quan vey cazer fuelhas e flors*', in *Neuphilologische Mitteilungen*, 64 (1963), 105–24 (here 119–20, ll. 9–16): 'E denant nos estai lo miradors / que fo a totz cominalmen donatz,/ Jherusalem, on Jhesus fon liatz / e receupt mort sus en la vera cros, / e·l cors pauzatz el verai monimen; / e fora bo que no fos oblidatz / tan ricx mirals qu'er breumen esfassatz / si no·l trazem foras de serva gen.' All translations are my own, unless otherwise stated.

[2] Key works include K. Lewent, 'Das altprovenzalische Kreuzlied', *Romanische Forschungen*, 21 (1905), 321–448; P. Hölzle, *Die Kreuzzüge in der okzitanischen und deutschen Lyrik des 12. Jahrhunderts: Das Gattungsproblem 'Kreuzlied' im historischen Kontext* (Göppingen, 1980); S. Guida (ed.), *Canzoni di Crociata* (Parma, 1992); L. Paterson, *Singing the Crusades: French and Occitan Lyric Responses to the Crusading Movements, 1137–1336* (Woodbridge,

2018), and the companion website 'Troubadours, Trouvères and the Crusades' (https://www.warwick.ac.uk/crusadelyrics).

3   On the influence of the lyric on the wider public, see, for example, S. Guida, 'Canzoni di crociata ed opinione pubblica del tempo', in A.-M. Babbi et al. (eds), *Medioevo romanzo e orientale: Testi e prospettive storiographiche* (Soveria Mannelli, 1992), pp. 41–52; M. Aurell, 'Les troubadours: naissance et diffusion de la chanson engagée', in L. Vadelorge and L. Tournés (eds), *Les sociabilités musicales: sociabilité, culture et patrimoine* (Rouen, 1997), pp. 25–36; S. Vatteroni, 'Verbum exhortationis e propaganda nella poesia provenzale del XIII secolo', in R. Castano, F. Latella and T. Sorrenti (eds), *Comunicazione e propaganda nel secoli XII e XIII* (Rome, 2007), pp. 653–79.

4   There is, however, debate surrounding Raymond IV's influence in the Latin East. See, for example, K. Lewis, *The Counts of Tripoli and Lebanon in the Twelfth Century: Sons of Saint-Gilles* (Abingdon, 2017), and T. Lecaque, 'The Count of Saint-Gilles and the Saints of the Apocalypse: Occitanian Piety and Culture in the Time of the First Crusade' (unpublished PhD dissertation, University of Tennessee, Knoxville, 2015). See more generally M. Barber, *The Crusader States* (New Haven, CT, 2012).

5   Aimeric de Belenoi, *Consiros, com partis d'amor*, ed. C. Menichetti, <http://www.rialto.unina.it/AimBel/9.10/9.10%28Menichetti%29.htm> (last accessed 25 Jan 2019), (lines 19–21): 'Que·l conquist que nostr'ansesor / conqueiron en Terra Major / perdem...'

6   Peirol, *Pus flum Jordan ai vist e·l monimen*, ed. R. Harvey, <http://www.rialto.unina.it/Peirol/366.28/366.28%28Harvey%29.htm> (last accessed January 2019), lines 15–16: 'Qu'Englaterra a croy emendamen/ del rey Richart...'

7   N. Paul, *To Follow in their Footsteps: The Crusades and Family Memory in the High Middle Ages* (Ithaca, NY, 2012).

8   Paul, *To Follow in their Footsteps*, pp. 128–33.

9   C. Gaposchkin, 'The Echoes of Victory: Liturgical and Para-Liturgical Commemorations of the Capture of Jerusalem in the West', *Journal of Medieval History*, 40/3 (2014), 237–59 (here 241–2).

10 A. Linder, *Raising Arms: Liturgy in the Struggle to Liberate Jerusalem in the Middle Ages* (Turnhout, 2003).

11 Linder, *Raising Arms*, pp. 28–9.

12 Paterson, *Singing the Crusades*, pp. 47–75.

13 Bertran de Born, *Nostre Seigner somonis el meteis*, ed. G. Gouiran, in *L'amour et la guerre: L'oeuvre de Bertran de Born*, 2 vols (Aix-en-Provence, 1985), vol. 2, p. 666 (ll. 1–6): 'Nostre Seigner somonis el meteis / totz los ardiz e·ls valens e·ls prezatz, / q'anc mais guerra ni cocha no·l destreis, / Mas d'aqesta si ten fort per grevatz; / Qar presa es la vera crotz e·l reis, / e·l sepolcres ha de socors fraichura.'

14 Peire Vidal, *Anc no mori per amor ni per al*, ed. D. S. Avalle, in *Peire Vidal: Poesie*, 2 vols (Milan, 1960), vol. 2, pp. 333–6 (ll. 49–56): 'Lai vir mon chan, al rei celestial, / cui devem tug onrar et obezir, / et es mestier que l'anem lai servir, / on conquerrem la vid' esperital; / que·lh Sarrazi, deslial Caninieu, / l'an tout son rengn'e destruita sa plieu, / que sazit an la crotz e·l monimen: / don devem tug aver gran espaven.'

15 *Poésies complètes du troubadour Peire Cardenal (1180–1278)*, ed. R. Lavaud (Toulouse, 1957), p. 180.

16 *Il trovatore Peire Cardenal*, ed. S. Vatteroni, 2 vols (Modena, 2013), vol. 1, p. 299. I cite Vatteroni's edition of *Dels quatre caps*, vol. 1, pp. 303–5.

17 *Peire Cardenal*, ed. Vatteroni, vol. 1, pp. 303–5 (ll. 8–9): 'La crotz es lo dreitz gonfanos/ del rei cui tot cant es apen.'

18. *Peire Cardenal*, ed. Vatteroni, vol. 1, p. 306. See also G. Constable, 'Jerusalem and the sign of the cross (with particular reference to the cross of pilgrimage and crusading in the twelfth century)', in L. Levine (ed.), *Jerusalem: Its Sanctity and Centrality to Judaism, Christianity, and Islam* (New York, 1999), pp. 371–81 (here pp. 372-4); B. Baert, *A Heritage of Holy Wood: The Legend of the True Cross in Text and Image*, trans. L. Preedy (Leiden, 2004), pp. 2–3, 71–2, and *passim*.
19. D. Gerish, 'The True Cross and the Kings of Jerusalem', *Haskins Society Journal*, 8 (1996), 137–42; A. V. Murray, '"Mighty against the enemies of Christ": the relic of the True Cross in the armies of the kingdom of Jerusalem', in J. France and W. Zajac (eds), *The Crusades and Their Sources: Essays Presented to Bernard Hamilton* (Aldershot, 1998), pp. 217–38.
20. M. Cassidy-Welch, 'Before Trauma: The Crusades, Medieval Memory and Violence', *Continuum*, 31/5 (2017), 619–27 (here 621).
21. *Peire Cardenal*, ed. Vatteroni, vol. 1, pp. 303–5 (ll. 36–7): '. . . qui la cros pren/e siec Crist ves on que tenha.'
22. Compare, for example, Gregory VIII's encyclical, *Audita Tremendi*, issued in response to Hattin: 'We therefore should heed and be concerned about the sins not only of the inhabitants of that land but also of our own and those of the whole Christian people . . .' Translation from J. Bird, E. Peters and J. Powell (eds), *Crusade and Christendom: Annotated Documents in Translation from Innocent III to the Fall of Acre, 1187–1291* (Philadelphia, PA, 2013), p. 7.
23. *Poésies complètes*, ed. Lavaud, p. 182.
24. L. Macé, *Les comtes de Toulouse et leur entourage (XIIe–XIIIe siècles): rivalités, alliances et jeux de pouvoir* (Toulouse, 2000), pp. 97–146.
25. Key works on troubadour responses to the Albigensian Crusade include, E. Miruna Ghil, *L'Age de Parage: Essai sur le poétique et le politique en Occitanie au XIIIe siècle* (New York, 1989); M. Aurell, *La Vielle et l'épée: troubadours et politique en Provence au XIIIe siècle* (Paris, 1989); S. Vatteroni, *Falsa Clercia: la poesia anticlericale dei trovatori* (Alessandria, 1999); J. Puckett, '"Rencomenciez Novele Estoire": The Troubadours and the Rhetoric of the Later Crusades', *Modern Language Notes*, 116/4 (2001), 844–89; Paterson, *Singing the Crusades*, pp. 123–35, 154–66.
26. Peire Cardenal, *Si tot non ai ioy ni plazer*, in *Peire Cardenal*, ed. Vatteroni, vol. 2, pp. 660–2 (ll. 49–50): 'e·l Sepulcres es del tot oblidatz / e la terra on Iesu Crist fon natz'.
27. I. Frank, 'Tomier e Palaizi, troubadours tarasconais', *Romania*, 78 (1957), 46–85 (here 74) (ll. 18, 45): 'falsa croisada', 'fals nesci sout'.
28. Guilhem Figueira, *D'un sirventes far*, ed. G. Peron, <http://www.rialto.unina.it/GlFig/217.2/217.2%28Peron%29.htm> (last accessed 25 January 2019), (ll. 67–70): 'Roma, als Sarrazis / faitz vos pauc de dampnatge, / mas Grecs e Latis / liuratz a carnalatge.'
29. G. Constable, *Three Studies in Medieval Religious and Social Thought: The Interpretation of Mary and Martha, the Ideal of the Imitation of Christ, the Orders of Society* (Cambridge, 1995), pp. 179–221; R. Fulton, *From Judgment to Passion: Devotion to Christ and the Virgin Mary, 800–1200* (New York, 2002), pp. 142–92; S. McNamer, *Affective Meditation and the Invention of Medieval Compassion* (Philadelphia, 2010).
30. Constable described these early depictions of the crucified Christ as showing a saviour 'indifferent to suffering'; Constable, *Three Studies*, p. 157.
31. C. Maier, *Crusade Propaganda and Ideology: Model Sermons for the Preaching of the Cross* (Cambridge, 2000); W. Purkis, *Crusading Spirituality in the Holy Land and Iberia, c. 1095–c. 1187* (Woodbridge, 2008).
32. Puckett, '"Rencomenciez Novele Estoire"'.
33. Paterson, *Singing the Crusades*, pp. 62–75.

34 M. Raguin-Barthelmebs, 'The words to say it: the crusading rhetoric of the troubadours and trouvères', in Paterson, *Singing the Crusades*, pp. 259–85 (here pp. 260–1).

35 Peire d'Alvernhe, *Lauzatz sia Hemanuel*, ed. A. Fratta, in *Peire d'Alvernhe: Poesie* (Rome, 1996), pp. 140–3, l. 15: 'pres per nos passio'.

36 Peire d'Alvernhe, *Cui bon vers agrada auzir*, ed. Fratta, in *Peire d'Alvernhe*, pp. 71–5, ll. 36–42: 'Ben deuria, pessan, morir / qui dregz huelhs garda sus lo vout, / cossi Dieus per nos a guerir / receup mort, e pus mort aucis / selhuy que per nos venc en crotz: / tug morrem, qu'avers non gueris / negun al temps plus que fes Iop.'

37 On the crucifix and devotion to Christ's humanity, see S. Lipton, '"The Sweet Lean of His Head": Writing about Looking at the Crucifix in the High Middle Ages', *Speculum*, 80/4 (2005), 1172–1208.

38 Bernart de Venzac, *Lo Pair'e·l Filh e·l Sant Espirital*, ed. M. P. Simonelli, in *Lirica moralistica nell'Occitania del XII secolo: Bernart de Venzac* (Modena, 1974), pp. 269–70 (ll. 29–35): 'Selh que per nos det son sanc natural / e se liuret e se mes en baylia, / et en la crotz fon levatz atretal / e clavellatz e coronatz d'espia, / nos don a far qu'al jorn del jutjamen / los nostres tortz no·l sia·n remembramen / ans ab gran gaug nos men en la su'alba.'

39 Pons de Capdoill, *So c'om plus vol e plus es voluntos*, ed. L. Mulholland, http://www.rialto.unina.it/PoChapt/375.22/375.22%28Mulholland%29.htm (last accessed 25 Jan 2019), ll. 9–16: 'Aras podem saber qu'El fetz per nos: / que'El se laisset d'espinas coronar, / batre e ferir e de fel abeurar, / e·ns rezemet del sieu sanc precios. / Ailias, chaitiu! Tant mal fant lor afaire / cill qui no·i van, e cuidon sai sostraire / a lor vezis las terras falsamen. / Paor deuran aver al jutgamen.'

40 Falquet de Romans, *Qan cuit chantar, eu plaing e plor*, ed. R. Arveiller and G. Gouiran, in *L'Oeuvre poétique de Falquet de Romans, troubadour* (Aix-en-Provence, 1987), pp. 88–92 (ll. 41–50): 'Ar prec al bon emperador / qi s'es croisaz per Deu servir / qe mueva ab força et ab vigor / ves la terra on Deus volc morir / e mes son cors en gage; / per nos en foi en croiz levaz / et es totz hom desesperaz / qi no·i a ferm corage / qi ve com el fo clavellaz / per nos e battuz e nafraz.'

41 Pujol, *Dieus es amors e verais salvamens*, Blacasset, *Se·l mals d'amor m'auzi ni m'es noisens*, Pujol, *Dieus es amors e verais salvamens*, Alaisina-Carenza, *Na Carenza al bel cors aveneç*, ed. P. di Luca, *Lecturae tropatorum*, 5 (2012), <http://www.lt.unina.it/DiLuca-2012.pdf> (last accessed 25 January 2019), ll. 22–3: 'e receup mort a tan gran viltenensa / e fon batutz si que·l sanc cazec jos'; Raimon Gaucelm de Béziers, *Qui vol aver complida amistansa*, ed. A. Radaelli, in *Raimon Gaucelm de Béziers: Poésie* (Florence, 1997), pp. 181–4 (ll. 9, 11–12): 'Dieus pres, per nos salvar, greu malanansa', 'que sus la crotz en volc penden murire / ab gran dolor ...'.

42 Guiraut Riquier, *Karitatz es amors e fes*, ed. M. Longobardi, 'I "vers" del trovatore Guiraut Riquier', *Studi mediolatini e volgari*, 29 (1982–3), 17–163 (here 65) (ll. 42–3): 'lo luecx on Jhesus Cristz fon natz / e visc e fon en crotz levatz'; Peire Cardenal, *De sirventes sueilh servir*, ed. Vatteroni, in *Peire Cardenal*, vol. 2, p. 325 (l. 30): 'Il luec on fom rezemut'; Bernart Alanhan de Narbona, *No puesc mudar qu'ieu non diga*, ed. L. Paterson, <http://www.rialto.unina.it/BnAlanh/53.1%28Paterson%29.htm> (last accessed 25 January 2019), (l. 36): 'on Dieus plors frays'.

43 Giraut de Borneil, *A l'honor Dieu torn en mon chan*, ed. R. Sharman, in *The Cansos and Sirventes of the Troubadour Giraut de Borneil* (Cambridge, 1989), pp. 414–17 (l. 61): 'Ben sapchatz que·m peza del dan.'

44 Giraut de Borneil, *Jois sia comensamens*, ed. Sharman in *Giraut de Borneil*, pp. 419–23, ll. 73–7: 'Per que·m par recrezemens, / si·l reis qu'es mager abdura los mals ni·ls deschauzimens, / qu'om sans ni valens / estei de l'anar duptos.'

[45] Bernart Alanhan de Narbona, *No puesc mudar qu'ieu non diga*, ed. and trans. Paterson, <*http://www.rialto.unina.it/BnAlanh/53.1%28Paterson%29.htm*> (last accessed 25 January 2019), (ll. 35–6): 'mas pauc vezem que negus bays / la crotz ploran on Dieus plors frays.' See also Paterson's notes regarding the dating of the lyric.

[46] P. Nagy, 'Religious weeping as ritual in the medieval West', in D. Handelman and G. Lindquist (eds), *Ritual in its Own Right: Exploring the Dynamics of Transformation* (New York, 2005), pp. 119–37; S. J. Spencer, 'The Emotional Rhetoric of Crusader Spirituality in the Narratives of the First Crusade', *Nottingham Medieval Studies*, 58 (2014), 57–86 (here 72–8).

'LI BONS DUS DE BUILLON': GENRE CONVENTIONS AND THE DEPICTION OF GODFREY OF BOUILLON IN THE *CHANSON D'ANTIOCHE* AND THE *CHANSON DE JÉRUSALEM*[1]

Simon John

The First Crusade (1095–9) exerted a profound cultural impact in Latin Christendom in the Middle Ages. Even before its forces had captured Jerusalem in July 1099, written reports and spoken traditions concerning the expedition had begun to circulate in the West, and both continued to do so in the centuries that followed.[2] As a result of this process, many of the expedition's participants – particularly its leaders – acquired great renown in Europe. Stories of their deeds were told and retold in the ensuing years, decades and centuries. Godfrey of Bouillon, the prominent leader who was appointed to rule the nascent state of Jerusalem soon after the Holy City's capture, became the nexus of a particularly rich constellation of traditions after his death in 1100.[3] By the turn of the fourteenth century, Godfrey had been transformed into an icon of the First Crusade, and of crusading more generally. It was the symbolic status that Godfrey had acquired by about 1300 that adduced Dante to include Godfrey as a 'warrior of the faith' in the *Divine Comedy*, and established the conditions in which Godfrey was enrolled into the roster of chivalric heroes known as the 'Nine Worthies'.[4] This article will consider an important dynamic of the process through which Godfrey was metamorphosed into a figure who, by the end of the thirteenth century, had come to embody aristocratic ideas and expectations.

Medieval traditions pertaining to the memory of Godfrey and the First Crusade took several different forms. From the first years of the twelfth century, a range of authors produced full-length narrative accounts of the expedition, working predominantly in Latin prose.[5] Alongside this surge in Latin historiography, there also took shape a body of vernacular rhymed songs concerning the First Crusade. At some point, these songs were given the form of Old French *chansons de geste*.[6] These crusade *chansons* probably existed in the twelfth century only as oral texts, and were only compiled into written form in the thirteenth century.[7] This body of *chansons* – known as the Crusade Cycle – collectively advances an embroidered and at points purely fictional rendition of the origins, history and aftermath of the First Crusade, conveying a narrative that is infused with the ethos of the martial aristocracy.[8] At the heart of the Crusade Cycle is a central trilogy of songs – the *Chanson d'Antioche*, the *Chanson des Chétifs* and the *Chanson de Jérsualem* – known as the 'cycle rudimentaire'.[9] The extant versions of this central trilogy were probably consolidated into their extant form in the late twelfth or early thirteenth century.[10] The *Chanson d'Antioche* focuses on the origin of the First Crusade and covers the expedition through to the aftermath of the capture of Antioch. The *Jérusalem* picks up the narrative of the First Crusade where the *Antioche* left off, covering the crusaders's attack on the Holy City, the appointment of Godfrey as its ruler, and the efforts by the crusaders to defend the city. *Les Chétifs*, whose events purport to have taken place between those of the *Antioche* and the *Jérusalem*, tells of the adventures of a trio of captured crusaders in the service of a Muslim potentate.[11]

Taking the Crusade Cycle as a whole, Godfrey functions as its main protagonist. This was an outcome of the way in which the cycle developed over time.[12] A branch of the cycle, probably composed in the first part of the thirteenth century to extend the narrative of the 'cycle rudimentaire' back in time, recounts a fictionalised and at points fantastical version of the history of Godfrey's family and exploits before the First Crusade, casting him as the scion of the legendary warrior known as the Swan Knight. A further body of late thirteenth-century songs picks up the narrative as it ended at the conclusion of the *Chanson de Jérusalem* to recount stories relating to the reigns of Godfrey's successors in the Holy City. Yet, a critical reading of the *Antioche* and *Jérusalem* in isolation from the remainder of the cycle indicates that Godfrey is not the unalloyed hero of these songs. The other chief participants in the First Crusade are depicted in a similarly exalted light. Indeed, references to Bohemond in the *Antioche* even outnumber those to Godfrey. In short, then, Godfrey was moulded into the main character of the Crusade Cycle through the addition of the *chansons* which focus on his ancestry and early life and those which purport to recount the deeds of his successors in Jerusalem.[13]

Unlike texts such as the *Chanson de Roland* and the other *chansons de geste* devoted to Charlemagne and his family and associates, which were composed three or four centuries after the events they purported to recount, the Crusade Cycle started to take shape within only about a century – perhaps three or four generations – of the First Crusade. Moreover, there are clear synergies between the extant versions of the *chansons* embedded in the Crusade Cycle and the Latin prose chronicles of the expedition.[14] While it may thus be tempting to mine these *chansons* for information about the historical crusade, and the activities of its participants, this is a temptation which is to be firmly resisted. By means of an analysis of the depiction of Godfrey of Bouillon in the *Chanson d'Antioche* and the *Chanson de Jérusalem*, the main songs of the 'cycle rudimentaire', and thus of the Crusade Cycle as a whole, and drawing from the work of scholars such as Noble and Hanley on the expectations and literary tropes which shaped the portrayals of main characters in the *chansons de geste*, this essay aims to show that the controlling principles which underpinned the depiction of Godfrey in these texts were the genre conventions of the *chansons*.[15] In short, these texts tell us nothing about the 'real' crusade, but instead give insight into how the memory of the expedition was shaped by aristocratic expectations concerning the heroes of the *chansons de geste*. It will be suggested that the *Antioche* and the *Jérusalem* are typical of the *chansons* in the sense that they utilise a variety of narrative strategies designed to present their protagonists in a particular light.

The article has three lines of inquiry in respect of the presentation of Godfrey in the *Antioche* and the *Jérusalem*. First, it will explore the emphasis placed on Godfrey's noble character, reputation and lineage. Second, it will consider the ways in which the songs accentuate his prowess as a man of war. Third, it will interrogate the methods used to portray him as a man devoted to the Christian faith. The essay will not consider every single reference to Godfrey in the texts, but it will draw from representative examples. It should be pointed out that in many of the instances in which Godfrey is referred to, the precise word formation seems to have been principally determined by the metre and rhyming scheme of the particular verse (*laisse*) in which the reference appears. Nevertheless, this supports the overarching argument of this essay: that the conventions of the genre play a key role in how Godfrey is portrayed in the *Antioche* and the *Jérusalem*.

Nobility was a key characteristic of the heroes of *chansons de geste*.[16] Throughout the two *chansons* under consideration here, Godfrey is repeatedly credited with noble characteristics. He is habitually referred to with an epithet or short phrase intended to underline his personal qualities. Hence, he is referred to in the *Antioche* in terms such as 'the good duke Godfrey'[17], 'the eminent Godfrey'[18], the 'lion-hearted duke'.[19] Likewise, in the *Jérusalem* he is variously referred to with closely related terms such as 'the good duke'[20] or 'the good Duke of Bouillon'.[21] A quality that is consistently imputed to Godfrey in these songs is that of bravery. This is perhaps to be expected, since personal courage was an essential attribute for the heroes of the *chansons*.[22] Hence, in the *Antioche*, he is described as 'the brave Godfrey of Bouillon'[23] and 'the brave-faced Godfrey'.[24] Similarly, the *Jérusalem* refers to Godfrey as 'lion-hearted'[25], 'valiant'[26], and asserts that he 'had the courage of a wild boar'.[27] A brief reference to Godfrey in the *Chétifs* ascribes similar qualities (*Godefrois a le chiere hardie*).[28] The *Antioche* and the *Jérusalem* also emphasise Godfrey's courage by according him particular feats of bravery. In addition to his various feats in battle (which are discussed in more detail below), it is recounted in the *Antioche* that Godfrey was chosen to be the crusaders' champion in an episode of single combat, in part because of his bravery.[29] His courage is depicted in contexts other than the battlefield; in one passage in the *Antioche*, Godfrey volunteers to keep guard over the crusader camp during the night, with only his own horse for company. The *Jérusalem* attributes a similar action to him.[30]

Heroes of *chansons* also possessed exemplary reputations. Both songs under consideration in this article thus seek to convey the sense that Godfrey had earned repute for carrying out noteworthy deeds. The very first reference to him in the *Antioche* casts him as a man 'with many achievements to his credit'.[31] In another passage, he is described simply as 'renowned' (*Godefrois l'alosés*).[32] Similarly, at one point in the *Jérusalem*, he is described as 'renowned for his achievements'.[33] In one of the few references to Godfrey in the *Chétifs*, he is called 'that author of noble deeds Duke Godfrey'.[34] At the point in the *Jérusalem* in which Godfrey is appointed 'king' of Jerusalem, it is related that he was 'the best knight who ever put on a sword'.[35]

Another important element in the depiction of heroes in the *chansons* is their lineage and family.[36] A significant passage in the *Antioche* is devoted specifically to Godfrey's ancestry. In that passage, Godfrey is chosen as the crusaders' champion in single combat in part because of his descent from Charlemagne (*k'il est . . . del linage Carlon*).[37] The ensuing verse then sets out in detail his proud lineage, pinpointing his descent from the legendary warrior known as the Swan Knight.[38] His connection to the Swan Knight is also referenced twice in the *Jérusalem*.[39] In line with this focus on Godfrey's lineage are repeated instances in which Godfrey is explicitly connected to his brothers, Baldwin and Eustace of Boulogne, who are also presented in positive terms. At one point the *Antioche* refers to Eustace as 'the brother of the duke of Bouillon'[40], while the *Jérusalem* calls Baldwin the same (*frere au duc de Bullon*).[41] One short *laisse* of the *Antioche* is devoted specifically to recounting a feat of arms carried out in one battle by Baldwin, closely followed by a deed enacted by Eustace.[42] In one military encounter related in the *Jérusalem*, Baldwin is described as declaiming that he was 'the brother of the valiant Duke Godfrey and the noble-hearted Count Eustace'.[43] In several instances in the *Jérusalem*, the three brothers are depicted acting – and often fighting – alongside one another. In one battle, for instance, the three brothers invoke Christ whilst swearing in unison that they would rather be decapitated than retreat even the length of a lance.[44] At another point, Godfrey calls out to his two brothers amidst a battle to encourage them: 'What are you playing at brothers? Come on, do not act like cowards. We are reputed to be the bravest in God's army: do not fear death, go out and seek it!'[45]

Another strategy employed to impute the connected qualities of lineage and nobility to Godfrey is apparent in passages in which he is depicted as a man concerned with these qualities in others. In the *Antioche*, Godfrey at one point greets William of Grandmesnil thus: 'How are things with you, noble baron's son?'[46] At another point, Godfrey is depicted commenting on a seneschal who had distinguished himself in one military engagement that, in the light of his exploits, 'he can be knighted whenever he wants'.[47] Godfrey is at another juncture in the *Antioche* used to vocalise praise of Robert of Flanders, asserting that he did not know 'anyone more noble in bearing arms'.[48] Similarly, at one point Godfrey addresses Robert of Normandy in the following terms: 'You are a noble count, a good man and brave with it'.[49] In the *Jérusalem*, Godfrey addresses Robert of Flanders in terms that accentuate his qualities (*Cosin, molt estes ber*).[50] When making a rousing speech to the rest of the crusading army to encourage them before the assault upon Jerusalem, he addresses them as 'noble lords and brave knights'.[51]

The *Antioche* and the *Jérusalem* place particular emphasis on Godfrey's many talents and qualities as a man of war, both as a leader of men and as a warrior in his own right. A key characteristic of a leader in the *chansons de geste* was the ability to inspire his men.[52] This no doubt informed the passages in which Godfrey is cast as an effective and energising general. At one point in the *Jérusalem*, he 'put heart into his men' with his war cry.[53] At one juncture in the *Antioche*, Godfrey exhorts the crusaders to fight their Turkish enemy, and they respond to him that they would follow him to the death.[54] Ahead of another battle, Godfrey makes an exhortation to his men not to lose heart, prompting them to respond: 'My Lord, we shall do as you command … All of us would rather die than do anything shameful.'[55] At the end of the *Antioche*, when it is reported to the rest of the leaders that Godfrey had gone missing after the major battle outside Antioch, they are described as bursting into tears, before mounting a rescue mission: 'If we cannot get him back, we shall follow after him all the way to the kingdom of Persia.'[56] In the *Jérusalem*, when the crusaders arrive at the Holy City, Thomas of La Fère outlines how the commanding fortifications of the city make it such a difficult military target, but asserts that he would attack the city with all his might 'by the loyalty I owe Godfrey of Bouillon and Our Lord whom I love and adore.'[57] Ahead of another battle in this song, Peter the Hermit affirms his personal commitment to Godfrey as follows: 'My lord, I am going to take up arms too in recognition of the love I bear you.'[58] After Godfrey's appointment as 'king' of Jerusalem, he makes a speech exhorting his men the day before they were to ride to battle. The crusader forces offer the following reply: 'King Godfrey, our lord, you are our protector and not one of us will let you down even at the price of dismemberment. Every last one would rather have his head cut off than flee as much as four feet from the pagans.'[59]

Noble's study of the qualities associated with military leaders in the *chansons* indicates that strategic sense was not as critical a characteristic as personal bravery.[60] However, this is not to suggest that strategic sense was an insignificant quality for the chief protagonists. It is the case that the songs of the 'cycle rudimentaire' at certain points emphasise Godfrey had knowledge of military tactics. Hence, at one point in the *Antioche*, he is depicted instructing Stephen of Blois to lead a force to guard a mountain pass, while the *Jérusalem* has Godfrey drawing up the crusaders' battle lines ahead of their assault on the Holy City.[61] Moreover, Godfrey is held up as a shrewd tactician, a man who was capable of enacting elaborate tricks which effectively fooled the crusaders' enemies. At one juncture in the *Jérusalem*, the crusaders intercept carrier pigeons sent by the Muslim ruler of Jerusalem. The pigeons were carrying messages which requested other Muslim lords in the region to send reinforcements. Godfrey is credited with the idea of replacing the original messages with letters encouraging Muslim armies to stay away from the Holy City.[62] Later on, after his appointment as 'king', Godfrey originates an even more elaborate ruse designed to bolster the crusaders' chances while they were besieged inside the Holy City. The song states that Godfrey, a 'shrewd operator' had each of his force of 20,500 men march past the enemy army ten times, changing his clothes after each pass. The song suggests that this 'remarkably cunning trick' successfully fooled the besieging army into thinking that the crusader army was larger than it was.[63]

The *chansons de geste* typically devote close attention to the items used by their heroes in warfare. Weapons (especially swords) and armour are often described as exhibiting exquisite craftsmanship as well as having exotic and prestigious origins. As Hanley notes, these descriptions of arms and armour essentially function as self-contained narrative elements within the texts.[64] Linked to this, the *chansons* regularly contain highly formulaic scenes in which the leading protagonists ritually arm themselves ahead of battle. The *Jérusalem* thus provides descriptions of Godfrey's flag – 'a dragon which had a diagonal pattern on its tail'[65] – and his tent.[66] One arming scene in the *Antioche* recounts how Godfrey took up his hauberk and sword before mounting his Gascon warhorse.[67] In another arming scene later in the same song, Godfrey is aided by the otherwise unknown Antelm of Avignon (who laced his greaves for him), before donning his hauberk, his round helmet, his sword, and mounting his horse (on this occasion a steed from Carion).[68] In one particularly crucial arming scene in the *Antioche*, Godfrey is assisted in his pre-battle rituals by his brothers:

> [Godfrey] put on his greaves and hauberk. Baldwin and Eustace laced up his helmet; then he buckled on his prized sword. Shield round his neck, he swung into Capalu's saddle. There were four dragons on the flag he carried. Once [Godfrey] was armed he spurred his horse on so powerfully that it arched its back beneath him'.[69]

The significance of arms and armour in these songs is also attested by the passage in the *Jérusalem* in which the 'sultan of Persia' sends Godfrey a messenger on a fine white Aragonese horse, with a fine saddle and valuable decorated stirrups, in an effort to tempt and distract Godfrey, and thereby undermine his ability to fight.[70] Godfrey, though, does not take the bait. It is also of note that the songs relate that Godfrey used a number of different horses throughout the crusade. In addition to the aforementioned Gascon warhorse and his steed from Carion, he variously rides an 'excellent Syrian mule'[71], an Arab warhorse,[72] a Castilian horse,[73] and a 'white horse from Alenie'.[74] Whilst these different mounts no doubt serve to perpetuate the rhyming scheme of the particular *laisse* in which they each appear, they nonetheless convey the impression that Godfrey had a different horse for almost every military encounter.

The songs also depict Godfrey as a man who was constantly thirsty for battle. Hence, in one passage in the *Antioche*, when the bishop of Le Puy asks Godfrey to carry the Holy Lance into battle, he refuses in the following terms: 'I would not carry it even if you were to give me all the gold in Russia. I am more interested in fighting the hated [Saracens] . . . I shall strike so many blows with my glittering sword that my entire fists will be blackened with [their] blood.'[75] In the same song, while the crusaders are taunted by the foe known as Brohadas at Antioch, Godfrey is said to have 'thought it inexcusable not to go and strike him'.[76] In the *Jérusalem*, as the crusaders were preparing to make their assault on the Holy City, it is related that Godfrey 'did not hang back: he had the great horn blown aloud. This was a signal for those in the army to arm themselves.'[77]

More than anything else, the *chansons de geste* are concerned with recounting warfare itself. They have a particular focus on battles, and above all episodes of single combat between Christian heroes and their 'pagan' adversaries. These set-piece one-on-one encounters are a principal mechanism for conveying knightly heroism, as well as a narrative device for conveying battle scenes in the context of oral delivery.[78] What elevates the heroes from the rest of the Christian protagonists in the *chansons* is the fact that they possess superhuman strength and skill, and above all the ability to inflict devastation upon the enemy lines – as well as individual foes – in combat.[79] For this reason, particular attention is paid to Godfrey's talent with the sword in the 'cycle rudimentaire'. At one point in the *Antioche*, Godfrey stands guard alone during the night, and, after being attacked, is described as decapitating fourteen enemy warriors, with the rest of his comrades learning of his feat only when they rose from their beds the next morning.[80] Later on in the song, he decapitates a foe named Soliman with his sword.[81] He is at one point described as being separated from the rest of the crusaders and fighting hordes of enemies on his own (a common plot device in the *chansons*).[82]

In that passage, he is described as wreaking havoc, with the narrator comparing him to other heroes found in other cycles of *chansons de geste*: 'Anyone who could have seen [Godfrey] dismembering Saracens and sending one of top of another somersaulting dead to the ground would have had no need to invoke the memory of Bertrand [of Orange] or Aimeri [of Narbonne].'[83] At another point, Godfrey strikes another unfortunate foe with such venom that he 'sliced his heart in two inside his chest'.[84]

One passage in the *Jérusalem* calls on its audience to imagine Godfrey 'dealing out death and destruction, cutting off the heads of more than 20,000 pagans'.[85] A few *laisses* later, he is recounted as flinging himself into battle against a force of 60,000 Turks, again distinguishing himself:

> Imagine him laying about him left, right and centre. I can tell you this for certain: he did not land one single blow which did not kill a Saracen or his horse. The ranks thinned in front of him no matter which way he turned. The Turks scattered in front of him like larks in front of a sparrowhawk, not daring to come near him ... The Turks killed his horse beneath him. He leapt up from it, full of courage, grasping his shield and drawing his steel sword. Anyone who saw the lord slicing his way through Saracens, sending one staggering to his death on top of another one, could not have imagined a better knight.[86]

The heroes of the *chansons de geste* are regularly described as scything opponents in two with a single blow of their sword. Godfrey's ability to enact this feat is a recurring theme of both the *Antioche* and the *Jérusalem*.[87] In an important sequence of *laisses* in the *Antioche*, he slices a number of enemies in two in quick succession. Firstly, he is recounted as having 'sliced a Turk in half right down to his lungs so that one half hung down on each side of the saddle'.[88] Shortly after that, in what might be intended as a recapitulation of the same feat, Godfrey is described as striking a 'Saracen' atop his helmet, 'slicing downwards so far into his vital organs that the two halves hung right down to ground level'.[89] Immediately after this, he encounters another unfortunate foe, this time mounted, whom 'he slashed straight through the spine so that one half [of the foe] fell to the ground while the other half stayed in the golden saddle, the body gripping tight though the soul had gone, with the leg stiff as if it had been fixed in position.'[90] This feat of swordsmanship is echoed in the *Jérusalem*. At one point in that song, Godfrey is described as cutting an opponent named Malargu in half through the chest.[91] Soon afterwards, Godfrey agrees to enter single combat with a foe named Marbrin. Godfrey permits Marbrin to strike two blows before he retaliates. Though Godfrey is slightly wounded by Marbin's strikes, he is able to retaliate after the second. It is recounted that Godfrey swung his sword down 'as viciously as a wind in a storm and cut [Marbrin] in half all the way down to the felt pad of the saddle. God performed an extraordinary miracle because [Godfrey] cut the swift horse into two halves. He left horse and rider utterly destroyed on a hillock.'[92]

In these songs, Godfrey's superhuman ability as a warrior extends beyond his proficiency with the sword. Echoing the contemporary chroniclers' references to Godfrey's accomplishment with the crossbow, the *Jérusalem* recounts several feats of skill carried out by Godfrey with his bow.[93] At one point, he unleashes an arrow from his 'strong, tautly strung bow', and kills three kites with just a single arrow; the onlooking crusaders regard the feat as an omen from God, while it instils fear into the hearts of their enemies.[94] A few passages later, Godfrey is depicted using a Turkish bow effectively in the midst of battle.[95] At another point, he is depicted riding his horse faster than a crossbow bolt could fly.[96] He is also shown as possessing immense acuity in his hearing; at one point he and Tancred are described as hearing a battle on the other side of a nearby hill.[97] It is also the case that the heroes of the *chansons* are able to sustain serious (and seemingly fatal) wounds and bear the resultant pain and yet be able to continue fighting.[98] Thus in the *Antioche*, when Godfrey is fighting on his own after being separated from the rest of the crusaders, he is described as being hit by numerous arrows shot by the Turks, being wounded in the liver and lungs, and beginning to fear that he would die as a result.[99]

Personal piety is another crucial characteristic for the heroes of the *chansons de geste*. The leading protagonists had to give their trust and faith to God, and also possess a profound devotion to the Christian faith.[100] Accordingly, the songs of the 'cycle rudimentaire' lay much emphasis on Godfrey's devotion to Christianity and his relationship with God. Hence at one point in the *Antioche* he is described as Godfrey 'who led our army in the name of Almighty God the Redeemer'.[101] A few passages later in that song, when Godfrey hears that other crusaders have captured the cities of Tarsus and Mamistra, he is depicted raising 'his hands to heaven and [thanking] Almighty God who suffered for us'.[102]

During the assault on Antioch, it is reported to Godfrey that the rest of the leaders have gone missing. Godfrey, presuming they have been killed, laments and asserts that if only he had been with them, he would have protected them: 'my faith is so strong that it would have been enough to prevent their deaths; I would have put paid to even 20,000 Turks.'[103] In the *Jérusalem*, he is referred to at one point as 'Godfrey who places a profound trust in God'.[104] When explaining to the other leaders outside Jerusalem how to set up the siege of the city, Godfrey beseeches them as follows: 'In the name of God pay attention and I will explain how we can set about taking Jerusalem'.[105] At another point, Godfrey 'swore by the Holy Sepulchre, where he hoped to worship' that he would pursue his foe Cornumarant until he was able to kill him.[106]

As well as possessing a deep personal religious conviction, Godfrey is also repeatedly shown both calling for and receiving divine assistance in battle. In the *Antioche*, after severely inclement weather weakens their assault on Antioch, Godfrey assures his crusaders that God will intervene to aid them.[107] At a later point in the song, Godfrey asks Christ directly for help in capturing Antioch: 'Our glorious Lord and Father God, who allowed yourself to suffer on the Holy Cross for the salvation of your people, just as this is true – which I believe to beyond question – please grant that tonight we may take the city.'[108]

Likewise, at the outset of the *Jérusalem*, Godfrey calls for divine assistance to improve the crusaders' position: 'Radiant redeeming Father and Holy Lady Mary, who carried within you the Saviour of the world, come to our aid now!'[109] At one point, he affirms to Robert of Flanders that the crusaders 'will take [Jerusalem] at the pleasure of God and St Peter'.[110] Crucially, Godfrey does not only request divine assistance; at certain moments, he receives it. Hence, at one point in the *Antioche* he receives help in battle from Sts George and Demetrius.[111] There is a direct echo of this in the *Jérusalem*, where it is recounted at one point that in the grand battle which took place after the capture of Jerusalem, Godfrey received divine assistance from Sts George, Maurice, Demetrius and others, who brought a force of over 300,000.[112]

In both songs, Godfrey is selected as a mouthpiece for the 'prière du plus grand péril'. These are a staple element of *chansons de geste*, in which the knightly protagonists make an extended and heartfelt invocation to God.[113] Near the end of the *Antioche*, Godfrey is separated from the rest of his comrades and fears death, prompting him to utter the following prayer:

> Glorious Lord God, you brought back the body of St Lazarus from the dead with your blessing. The beautiful Mary Magdalen came so close to you in the house of Simon and sat at your feet on a low couch; she poured out so many tears from the depth of her heart that she washed your feet with them all over, then anointed them with balm in the goodness of her heart. That was a very wise thing to do and she was well rewarded: you pardoned her all her sins. Lord, just as this is true – as we sincerely believe – just so please save my body from death and captivity and help me to avoid being overwhelmed by these wicked Saracens.[114]

In this instance, Godfrey's prayer is answered, for his fellow crusaders soon arrive to rescue him in the nick of time. In a very similar scene in the *Jérusalem* – so similar that it is to all intents and purposes a rerun of the scene in the *Antioche* just discussed – Godfrey makes another appeal for divine assistance, again in the form of a 'prière du plus grand péril', as follows: 'Lord God Our Father . . . take pity on the little army of Your people which has remained here to guard Your city where Your body suffered and the Holy Sepulchre in which You were laid.'[115]

This theme reaches its crescendo in the passage in the *Jérusalem* which recounts the circumstances in which Godfrey was chosen to be 'king' of Jerusalem. The song relates that the crusaders gathered in the Temple and beseeched God to indicate who should be granted the office. Then, at midnight, the crusaders are plunged into darkness, and there is a roll of thunder and a crash of lightning, which lights the previously unlit candle held by Godfrey, symbolising that he had been chosen by God to rule the Holy City. Godfrey promises to rule in Christ's name, and vouchsafes that he would give his life to protect the city if need be, prompting the rest of the crusaders to acclaim him: 'God has done a good day's work today in lighting his candle for you!'[116] Shortly before Godfrey's divine selection as 'king' in the *Jérusalem*, the song foreshadows his appointment by casting him as the conduit through which a miracle was enacted. In the passage recounting how the crusaders overran the city, Godfrey, along with Robert of Flanders and Thomas of Marle, is described as heading straight to the church of the Holy Sepulchre in order to begin cleaning it. Godfrey then encounters the warden of a nearby palace and throws the silken cloth with which he had cleaned the sepulchre onto the man's face, to signal he would take the keeper into his protection. The man, who has been unable to see for thirty years, instantly has his sight restored. Upon hearing this, Godfrey gives thanks to God.[117]

Crucially, at points in these songs, the depiction of Godfrey moves beyond the emphasis on his personal piety and divine sponsorship. In several important passages, he is used as the mouthpiece for vocalising the aims of the First Crusade and the beliefs of its participants. Hence, at one point in the assault on Jerusalem, Godfrey explains to the rest of the crusaders why they sought the city: 'Here is the city where God suffered death and lived again.'[118] At another point in the *Jérusalem*, when it seemed as though Peter the Hermit was close to death at the hands of the Turks, Godfrey spoke to encourage his men by telling them they were carrying out God's work: 'If you hold fast to your faith God will be your Defender: and if he comes to your aid you have nothing to fear.'[119] Shortly after, he again speaks to his men, and affirms that they need not fear death because of the spiritual rewards that awaited them if they were killed: 'Happy the one who dies for God; he will be crowned in Heaven with the angels.'[120] Shortly after this, an entire *laisse* is devoted to a prayer delivered by Godfrey directly to God, in which he shows a not inconsiderable understanding of biblical history and theology, before requesting that God send him a signal that he will defeat his enemies.[121]

This article has aimed to show how textual conventions of the *chansons de geste* played a key role in shaping how Godfrey of Bouillon was presented in both the *Chanson d'Antioche* and *Chanson de Jérusalem*. It shows that, in line with how the heroes of the *chansons* are generally depicted, great emphasis is placed on Godfrey's noble character, reputation and lineage, on his talents as a man of war, and as a man devoted to the Christian faith. However, in closing, it is important to note that these different facets were of course connected. The characteristics and qualities attributed to him must have been intended to mutually strengthen each other to advance an overall picture of a profoundly pious, militarily accomplished and noble warrior. This synergy is apparent at certain points: hence, at one point in the *Jérusalem*, Godfrey invokes Charlemagne's famous war-cry, before calling for aid in way which emphasises the underlying religious motivation of the First Crusade: 'Montjoie! Help us, Holy Sepulchre!'[122] In another passage, Godfrey speaks words directly to his sword that typify the different qualities: 'Sword . . . yet again I shall see you stained with the blood of dead Saracens. I shall go down fighting before I die if such be the pleasure of God and his mother, whose soul will be blessed.'[123] The incarnation of

Godfrey in the *Antioche* and the *Jérusalem*, then, tells us less about the 'real' Godfrey than it does about how the aristocratic preoccupations of the *chansons de geste* shaped the transmission of his memory.

Notes

1. All translations are from the following works: *ChAnt* from *The Chanson d'Antioche: An Old French Account of the First Crusade*, trans. S. B. Edgington and C. Sweetenham (Farnham, 2011); *Chétifs* from *The Chanson des Chétifs and Chanson de Jérusalem: Completing the Central Trilogy of the Old French Crusade Cycle*, trans. C. Sweetenham (Farnham, 2016), pp. 67–172; *ChJér* from *Chanson des Chétifs and Chanson de Jérusalem*, (trans.) Sweetenham, pp. 173–353.
2. C. Sweetenham, 'What really happened to Eurvin de Créel's donkey? Anecdotes in sources for the First Crusade', in M. Bull and D. Kempf (eds), *Writing the Early Crusades: Text, Transmission and Memory* (Woodbridge, 2014), pp. 75–88; S. John, 'Historical Truth and the Miraculous Past: The Use of Oral Evidence in Twelfth-Century Historical Writing on the First Crusade', *English Historical Review*, 130/543 (2015), 263–301. On the First Crusade, see: J. France, *Victory in the East: A Military History of the First Crusade* (Cambridge, 1994).
3. S. John, *Godfrey of Bouillon: Duke of Lower Lotharingia, Ruler of Latin Jerusalem, c. 1060–1100* (Abingdon, 2018).
4. John, *Godfrey of Bouillon*, pp. 227–53, discusses the development of Godfrey's posthumous reputation in the twelfth and thirteenth centuries, and his incarnations in the *Divine Comedy* and as one of the 'Nine Worthies'.
5. S. Edgington, 'Reviewing the evidence', in J. Phillips (ed.), *The First Crusade: Origins and Impact* (Manchester, 1997), pp. 57–77; W. Purkis, 'Rewriting the history books: the First Crusade and the past', in Bull and Kempf (eds), *Writing the Early Crusades*, pp. 116–26.
6. C. M. Jones, *An Introduction to the Chansons de Geste* (Gainesville, 2014).
7. On the manuscripts of the cycle, see the essay by G. M. Myers in *OFCC*, vol. 1, pp. xiii–lxxxviii.
8. For a starting point, see: K.-H. Bender, and H. Kleber, *Le Premier Cycle de la Croisade: De Godefroy à Saladin, entre la chronique et la conte de fees (1100–1300)* (Heidelberg, 1986).
9. The article will draw from the edition of the *Antioche* by Duparc-Quioc and the translation by Edgington and Sweetenham, and the edition of the *Jérusalem* by Thorp and the translation of it by Sweetenham (see n. 1, above). The notes will each contain two citations: the first to the edition, the second to the translation.
10. On the composition and date of the 'cycle rudimentaire', see *Chanson d'Antioche*, trans. Edgington and Sweetenham, pp. 3–48.
11. P. Péron, 'La croisade des "chétifs": tradition et renouvellement de la perspective épique', *Romania*, 125/497–8 (2007), 87–117.
12. For comments on the depiction of Godfrey and his family in the Crusade Cycle, see: D. A. Trotter, 'L'ascendance mythique de Godefroy de Bouillon et le Cycle de la Croisade', in L. Harf-Lancner (ed.), *Métamorphose et bestiaire fantastique au moyen âge* (Paris, 1985), pp. 107–35; S. John, 'Godfrey of Bouillon and the Swan Knight', in S. John and N. Morton (eds), *Crusading and Warfare in the Middle Ages: Realities and Representations, Essays in*

Honour of John France (Farnham, 2014), pp. 129–42; G. H. M. Claassens, 'De Zwaanridder en Nijmegen: Brabantse politiek in de literatuur', in *Jaarboek Numaga*, 38 (1991), 19–40.
13 John, 'Godfrey of Bouillon and the Swan Knight'.
14 See, for instance: S. Edgington, 'Albert of Aachen and the chansons de geste', in J. France and W. G. Zajac (eds), *The Crusades and Their Sources: Essays Presented to Bernard Hamilton* (Aldershot, 1998), pp. 23–37; F. Andrei, 'Alberto di Aachen e la Chanson de Jérusalem', *Romance Philology*, 63/1 (2009), 1–69; N. Thorp, 'La *Chanson de Jérusalem* and the Latin chronicles', in P. E. Bennett, A. E. Cobby and J. E. Everson (eds), *Epic and Crusade: Proceedings of the Colloquium of the Société Rencesvals British Branch held at Lucy Cavendish College, Cambridge, 27–28 March 2004* (Edinburgh, 2006), pp. 153–71.
15 C. Hanley, *War and Combat 1150–1270: The Evidence from Old French Literature* (Cambridge, 2003); P. Noble, 'Military leadership in the Old French epic', in M. Ailes, P. E. Bennett and K. Pratt (eds), *Reading Around the Epic: A Festschrift in Honour of Professor Wolfgang Van Emden* (London, 1998), pp. 171–91; A. Leclercq, *Portraits croisés: l'image des Francs et des Musulmans dans les textes sur la Première Croisade. Chroniques latines et arabes, chansons de geste françaises des XIIe et XIIIe siècles* (Paris, 2010).
16 As the aptly named Noble put it, the leading protagonists are 'all ... noble and most of them of the highest nobility'; Noble, 'Military leadership', pp. 179–81. Cf. Hanley, *War and Combat*, p. 130: 'the principal chivalric attributes are status and prowess'.
17 *ChAnt*, l. 94/144: 'li bons dus Godefois'.
18 *ChAnt*, l. 114/154: 'Godefrois qui tant fait a loer'.
19 *ChAnt*, l. 158/172: 'li dus ... qui cuer ot de lyon'.
20 *ChJér*, 104/232: 'li bons dus'.
21 *ChJér*, 111/238: 'li bons dus de Buillon'.
22 Noble, 'Military leadership', pp. 176–9.
23 *ChAnt*, l. 191/187: 'Godefrois de Buillon li hardis'.
24 *ChAnt*, l. 261/224: 'Godefrois ... a le ciere hardie'.
25 *ChJér*, 93/223: 'cuer ot de lion'.
26 *ChJér*, 125/250: 'Godefroi qui molt a hardement'.
27 *ChJér*, 82/214: 'cuer ot de sengler'.
28 *Chétifs*, 3/67.
29 *ChAnt*, l. 371/277.
30 *ChAnt*, l. 157–8/172; *ChJér*, 29/190.
31 *ChAnt*, l. 21/102: 'Godefroid ki molt fist a proisier'.
32 *ChAnt*, l. 62/129.
33 *ChJér*, 140/161: 'a la chiere menbree'.
34 *Chétifs*, 12/75: 'Godefroi, qui tant fait a douter'.
35 *ChJér*, 152/272: 'Del mellor chevalier qui ainc çainsist d'espee'.
36 Noble, 'Military leadership', p. 175.
37 *ChAnt*, l. 371/277.
38 *ChAnt*, l. 371–3/277–8.
39 *ChJér*, 212/318, 224/328.
40 *ChAnt*, l. 307/248: 'frere al duc de Bullon'.
41 *ChJér*, 64/199.
42 *ChAnt*, l. 85–6/140.
43 *ChJér*, 125/250: 'Frere au duc Godefroi qui molt a hardement / Et le conte Ewistace qui molt a le cors gent'.
44 *ChJér*, 164/281.

45 *ChJér*, 165/282: 'Que faites vos, mi frere? Ne vos alés faignant! / On dist que de l'ost Deu estiemes mius Vaillant. / Ne dotés pas le mort mais alés le querant!'
46 *ChAnt*, l. 139/165: 'Comment avés erré, gentius fils a baron?'.
47 *ChAnt*, l. 175/180: 'Quele hore qu'il vaurra chevalier en feron'.
48 *ChAnt*, l. 302/246: 'Je ne sai plus praudome por ses armes porter.'
49 *ChAnt*, l. 373/278: 'Robert, jentius quens, frans hon, ciere hardie'.
50 *ChJér*, 88/219.
51 *ChJér*, 137/259: 'gentius barnages! franc chevalier vaillant!'
52 Noble, 'Military leadership', pp. 181-2.
53 *ChJér*, 164/281: 'Godefrois a se gent resbaudie'.
54 *ChAnt*, l. 299/244.
55 *ChAnt*, 1. 396/289: 'Sire, vostre commant feron, / Miux volons tot morir que faire mesprison.'
56 *ChAnt*, 1. 455/317: 'Se nos nel retrovon / Dusqu'el regne de Perse aprés lui en iron.'
57 *ChJér*, 60/194: 'par le foi que doi Godefroi de Baiviere / Et la nostre segnor qui jo ainm et tieng ciere.'
58 *ChJér*, 185/298: 'Sire, por vostre amor serai jo armés ja.'
59 *ChJér*, 204/312: 'Sire, rois Godefrois, tu iés nos avoués, / Ja ne t'en faura uns por estre desmenbrés. / N'i a cel ne vausist mius fust ses ciés colpes / K'il fuïst por paiens .IIII. piés mesurés.'
60 Noble, 'Military leadership', pp. 182-9.
61 *ChAnt*, 1. 86-7/140; *ChJér*, 82-3/214-15.
62 *ChJér*, 97-100/227-8.
63 *ChJér*, 176/291: 'Godefrois fu hom de grant escïent . . . çou fu molt grans voisdie'.
64 Hanley, *War and Combat*, pp. 147-51.
65 *ChJér*, 208/314: 'Al tragon qui avoit la coue gironee'.
66 *ChJér*, 117/243.
67 *ChAnt*, 1. 158/172.
68 *ChAnt*, 1. 199/191.
69 *ChJér*, 211/317: 'Il a cauciés ses cauces, son auberc endossa. / Bauduïns et Wistases son elme le laça, / Puis a çainte l'espee que molt forment ama. / Son escu a son col en Chapalu monta, / En l'ensegne qu'il porte .IIII. dragons i a. / Quant li rois fu armés el ceval s'afiça/ Par issi grant vertu que sous lui arçoia.'
70 *ChJér*, 195-6/305-6.
71 *ChAnt*, 1. 373/279: 'del bon mul de Surie'.
72 *ChAnt*, 1. 434/308.
73 *ChJér*, 76/209.
74 *ChJér*, 244/343: 'le blanc d'Alenie'.
75 *ChAnt*, 1. 386/284: 'Sire . . . jo n'en porterai mie / Se vos or me doniés tot l'or qu'ist en Rosie. / Plus desir la bataille contre la gent haïe / . . . Tant i ferrai anqui de l'espee forbie / Que trosqu'en mes poins ert de lor sanc ennoircie.' The other leaders also make similar refusals to the bishop of Le Puy.
76 *ChAnt*, 1. 434/308: 'se ferir ne la va, tient soi a mal bailli'.
77 *ChJér*, 134/257: 'Godefrois . . . ne se vaut atargier,/ Le maistre cor a fait soner et grailloier. / Dont s'armerent par l'ost.'
78 Hanley, *War and Combat*, pp. 117-30.
79 Noble, 'Military leadership', pp. 175-82.
80 *ChAnt*, 1. 157-8/172.
81 *ChAnt*, 1. 444/312.
82 *ChAnt*, 1. 453-5/315-16.

83 *ChAnt*, 1. 445/317: 'Ki dont veïst le prince Sarrasins desmembre, / L'un mort deserve l'autre a terre trestorner, / Por nïent ramentust Bertran ne Aïmer.'
84 *ChAnt*, 1. 434/308: 'Le cuer qu'il a el ventre li a parmi parti.'
85 *ChJér*, 139/261: 'Mais li dus de Buillon lor fu a l'encontrer. Illuec le veïssiés molt fierement capler, / Plus de .XX.M. paiens fist les testes colper.'
86 *ChJér*, 166–7/283: 'Dont veïssiés le roi bien ses cols emploier. / Onques n'i feri coup – bien le puis afficier / – N'ocesist Sarrasin, u lui u son destrier. / Quel part que li rois torne fait les rens claroier. / Autresi con l'aloë fuit devant l'esprevier / Vont li Turc entor lui: ne l'osent aproismier … Car Turc lu onto cis desous lui son destrier; / Et li rois resaut sus, qui le corage ot fier, / Il embrasce l'escu et trait le brant d'acier. / Ki veïst le baron Sarrasins destrenchier / L'un mort desore l'autre abatre et trebucier, / Por nient ramenteüst nul mellor chevalier.'
87 On the ubiquity of the bisection feat in the *chansons*, and the various textual incarnations of Godfrey's reputed feat, see: S. John, '"Claruit ibi multum dux Lotharingiae": the development of the epic tradition of Godfrey of Bouillon and the bisected Turk', in S. Parsons and L. Paterson (eds), *The Literature of the Crusades* (Woodbridge, 2018), pp. 7–24.
88 *ChAnt*, ll. 200–1/192: 'Tot en fendi un Turc desci que el pomon, / Que le moitiés en pent d'ambes pars de l'arçon.'
89 *ChAnt*, 1. 201/192: 'Tout le fendi le cors desci qu'en la coree, / Que les motiés en pendent tot contreval la pree.'
90 *ChAnt*, 1. 202/193: 'Tot le coupa li dus tres parmi l'eskinee, / L'une moitiés des Turc caï emmi la pree, / Et li autre est remese en la sele doree, / Li cars del Turc s'estraint, car l'arme en est alee, / Si fu roide la jambe com s'ele fust plantee.'
91 *ChJér*, 189/301.
92 *ChJér*, 200/309: 'Si vait bruiant l'espee que vens encontré oré, / Dusqu'en l'afeutreüre l'a fendu et coupé. / Çou fu molt grans miracle que Dex i a mostré, / Car e[n] .II. motiés trence le destrier sejorné. / Tout abat en .I. mont et a jus craventé.'
93 On Godfrey's proficiency with the crossbow: John, *Godfrey of Bouillon*, pp. 56, 129, 162.
94 *ChJér*, 67/201: 'Li dus tenoit .I. arc fort et roit et traiant.'
95 *ChJér*, 85–6/217.
96 *ChJér*, 122/247.
97 *ChAnt*, 1. 94/144.
98 Noble, 'Military leadership', p. 175.
99 *ChAnt*, 1. 455–6/317. One might tentatively term this the 'Boromir effect'.
100 Noble, 'Military leadership', p. 189.
101 *ChAnt*, 1. 114/155: 'Qui nostre ost encounduist el non al raemant'.
102 *ChAnt*, 1. 139/165: 'Quant Godefrois l'oï, s'en tent ses mains amon, / Damedeu en gracie qui vint a passion.'
103 *ChAnt*, 1. 312/250–1: 'Jo me fi tant en Deu qu'il n'i morroient mie, / Si eüst ains des Turs .xx. mil tolu la vie.'
104 *ChJér*, 45/182: 'Godefrois, qui en Diu molt se fie.'
105 *ChJér*, 62/196: 'Or esgardés por Deu conment nos le feron, / Par con faite maniere Jursalem asauron.'
106 *ChJér*, 123/247: 'Et jure le Sepucre, qu'il vauroit aorer.'
107 *ChAnt*, 1. 191–2/187–8.
108 *ChAnt*, 1. 302/246: 'Glorious sire pere qui te laisas pener / En le saintime crois por ton pule salver, / Diex, si com ce est voirs, et jel croi sans douter, / Si nos donés a nuit le cité conquester.'

[109] *ChJér*, 38/176: 'Biaus pere raemans, / Sainte Marie dame, qui portas en tes flans / Le Salveor del mont, soiés nos hui aidans.'
[110] *ChJér*, 116/242: 'Se Deu plaist et saint Piere adonques le prendron.'
[111] *ChAnt*, 1. 158/172.
[112] *ChJér*, 166–7/283.
[113] On the nature of these prayers in general, see J. de Caluwé, 'La "prière épique" dans les plus anciennes chansons de geste françaises', *Olifant*, 4/1 (1976), 4–20.
[114] *ChAnt*, 1. 456/317–18: 'Glorieus sire pere, par vo beneïçon / De la mort surescistes le cors saint Lazeron; / Marie Madeleine a le gente façon / S'aproisma tant de vos a le maison Simon / Qu'ele vint a vos piés par desos un leson; / Des larmes de son cuer fist tel sorversion / Qu'ele les lava tos encoste et environ, / Aprés les oint de mire par bone entention, / Ele fist molt que sage, s'en ot bon gueredon, / Car de tos ses peciés li festistes pardon. / Sire, si com c'est voirs, et nos bien le creon, / Si garissiés mon cors de mort et de prison, / Que vaincre ne me puissant cist Sarrasin felon.'
[115] *ChJér*, 183/296: 'Segnor . . . se vos plaist, entendés! / Jou vos pri qu'il n'i ait .I. seul tant soit osés / Ki de la cité isse por cose que veés.'
[116] *ChJér*, 152/272: 'Bien a hui Dex por vos se candelle alumee.'
[117] *ChJér*, 144–5/265.
[118] *ChJér*, 85/217: 'Vés ici le cité u Dex ot mort et vie.'
[119] *ChJér*, 190/301: 'Bone creance aiés, Dex ert vos avoués: / Se il vos velt aidier ja mar vos douterés.'
[120] *ChJér*, 204/312: 'Cil qui por Deu morra ert molt bons eüres, / Et ciel avoec les angeles ert ses ciés coronés.'
[121] *ChJér*, 205–7/313–14.
[122] *ChJér*, 164/281: 'Monjoie! Sains Sepucres, aïe!'
[123] *ChJér*, 184/297: 'Espee . . . encore vos verrai tainte / De sanc Sarrasin dont la vie ert estainte. /Ançois que jo i muire i ferai tele empainte, / Se Deu plaist et sa mere, don't l'arme sere sainte.'

THE *GRAN CONQUISTA DE ULTRAMAR*, ITS PRECURSORS, AND THE LORDS OF SAINT-POL

Simon Thomas Parsons

The *Gran conquista de Ultramar* (hereafter *GCU*), best known after the 1503 printed edition (hereafter *GCU-S*) but referred to in the earliest manuscript as *Grant estoria de Ultramar*, is an extremely comprehensive compilatory history of the crusader states and the First Crusade, written in Old Castilian, and put together at the very end of the thirteenth century.[1] It covers events relating to Godfrey of Bouillon, the descendants of Charlemagne, and, most notably, the First Crusade and the Holy Land from the time of the emperor Heraclius to 1275. Presumably because of its length, language and the difficulties of its editorial history, it has not been used extensively as a historical source for the events of the crusade or the history of the crusader states, nor has it found much favour with literary scholars.[2] Besides, it is of comparatively late date and the narrative follows closely a combination of Old French texts, including the *Estoire d'Eracles* (the Old French adaptation and continuation of William of Tyre) and texts of the Old French Crusade Cycle (*OFCC*), including the central *Antioche–Chétifs–Jérusalem* trilogy, and a version of the Swan Knight matter which narratively preceded it. Despite this, it also used some sources which have not been convincingly identified.[3] The result of this has been the postulation of a dizzying array of lost sources. This article does not offer an easy solution to this conundrum, made more challenging because the *GCU* seemingly used a range of epic vernacular texts in Old French and Occitan, and it does not signal when the source for a passage has switched. The present essay argues instead that to subdivide this material lacking a known source arbitrarily into different hypothetical 'regional' epics based purely on the heroes it foregrounds, as most scholars have done to date, is methodologically flawed. While it could well be accurate, this approach contains the germ of its own self-confirmation. Nevertheless, the *GCU* constitutes crucial testimony for one or several of the underlying vernacular traditions which have been the subject of considerable academic enquiry for at least the past two hundred years, and so any further progress on these vexed areas of research must take the testimony of the *GCU* into account. As a demonstration of the fruitfulness of such an approach, this article establishes two additional points: first, that the *GCU* shares some material with the Anglo-Norman *Siège d'Antioche*, which suggests a common textual or orally performed ancestor; and second, that the focus on the heroics of the lords of Saint-Pol is not a unique feature of the so-called 'Graindor of Douai' recension of the *Antioche*, and cannot consequently be used to date and situate this recension. Rather, it should be conceptualised as an influence further back in the textual development of the Old French crusade epic, probably around the middle of the twelfth century.

Despite over 170 years of scholarship on the vernacular First Crusade epic, several quite fundamental questions about the development of the texts remain unresolved, and some manifestations of these traditions remain without adequate editions, including the *GCU*.[4] Chief among these questions is the controversy over the composition of the *OFCC*, in particular one of its component works, the *Chanson d'Antioche*, part of the central *Antioche–Chétifs–Jérusalem* trilogy and usually considered to be the earliest part of the cycle.[5] Put simply, the *Antioche*, while being at points a direct parallel to certain Latin texts of the First Crusade, in particular the *Historia* of Robert the Monk (*c.* 1110), is a vastly expanded and largely unique account (insofar as is any narrative of the First Crusade, in a corpus so profoundly interwoven). In the prelude, present in some but not all of the cyclical manuscripts, a figure named Graindor of Douai is linked with the 'renouvellement' of a pre-existing song, which had its original beginning omitted by *novel jougleor* (translated by Edgington and Sweetenham as 'new-fangled *jongleurs*') when they recited it. Furthermore, at a single point, the *Antioche* introduces a claim that the song (the original?) was composed by one 'Richard the Pilgrim', 'Cil qui le cançon fist . . . Ricars li pelerins'.[6] But the wording of both of these attributions is vague, and it is not clear if they are meant to refer to the whole song. Extensive discussion has focused on the exact relationship of these figures to the text – considering one or other as an epic poet, crusader eyewitness, editor, patron, *remanieur*, and in the case of Graindor, literary vandal – but there is no certainty that Richard even existed, or whether Graindor should be associated with reworking just the *Antioche*, or the whole central trilogy, including the *Chétifs* and the *Jérusalem*.[7] The pertinent point for this article is that the *Antioche* was preceded by earlier versions with some coherence as either sung or written texts, and that one of these may have been linked to a figure known as Richard. Scholarly opinions have differed greatly on the tenability of reconstructing this proto-*Antioche* or adumbrating its content and style. On the one hand, Suzanne Duparc-Quioc embarked on a detailed hypothetical reconstitution of Richard's song, while the most recent study of the *Antioche* in English took the approach that studying the extant text as an artefact of (in the authors' opinion) the early thirteenth century without speculating unduly on its original form is a more productive analytical approach.[8] This is by no means the only controversial debate around precursors to vernacular epic First Crusade accounts. There may also have existed an earlier version of the *Jérusalem*.[9] The genesis of the *Chétifs* has its own uncertainties, as narratives of Christian captives in the pagan court circulated as early as the first decade of the twelfth century, while at least part of the extant text was probably patronised by Raymond of Poitiers, prince of Antioch (1136–49).[10] The Occitan *Canso d'Antioca*, referred to in the *Chanson de la croisade albigeois* but of which only a fragment ('the Madrid Fragment') now survives, is mostly lost and its full content a matter of speculation.[11] Furthermore, it was probably related to the mystical lost history of Gregory Bechada, a vassal of Gouffier of Lastours, written for the bishop of Limoges in the early twelfth century, referred to by Geoffrey of Vigeois in the early 1180s.[12] The Anglo-Norman *Siège d'Antioche*, a further vernacular epic account of the First Crusade composed probably in the late twelfth century, draws upon an underlying body of material which may potentially be associated with a proto-*Antioche*, or proto-*Antioca*.[13] Evidently, the prehistory of these vernacular texts remains far from clear. Yet since these precursor narratives manifestly circulated in either oral and written form, influenced the Latin histories, and constituted one of the primary means through which contemporaries conceptualised the crusading movement at a crucial moment in the development of the Holy War ideal, their elucidation continues to be an irresistible temptation to those who seek to understand twelfth-century crusade narrativisation.[14]

The *GCU*, as a compilation which seemingly used several no longer extant epic texts, holds the potential to cast further light on this nebulous tradition. Unfortunately, there is no complete extant manuscript of the *GCU*. However, four fragmentary manuscripts survive, covering scattered sections of the whole, rarely coinciding: Madrid, Biblioteca Nacional de España (BNE), MS 1187; BNE, MS 2454; BNE, MS 1920, and Salamanca, Biblioteca Universidad, MS 1698. Two of these fragments, MS 1920 (*c.* 1375–1425), and MS 2454 (fourteenth-century), contain sections from the portion of the *GCU* dealing with the First Crusade, and are thus relevant here.[15] Together, the manuscripts cover only around 73.5 per cent of the work.[16] The rest can only be established using *GCU-S*, whence the two fullest modern printed texts have taken the bulk of the text. However, there is no satisfactory scholarly edition of the *GCU*.[17] Pascual de Gayangos's edition used only *GCU-S* and MS 1187, and he gave no indication whence his readings derived, occasionally changing the orthography without alerting readers.[18] A lifelong project to edit the *GCU* by George Tyler Northup, active between 1919 and 1964, remains in typescript unpublished form in the University of Chicago Library Special Collections Research Centre, but he and his team did not know of MS 1920. Two microfiche 'texts' and concordances produced by the Hispanic Seminary of Medieval Studies in Madison give the testimonies of individual manuscripts and printed editions.[19] The full text of MS 1187 has been published in a separate volume.[20] A complete transcription of MS 2454 is given in a 1989 volume by Maria Theresa Echenique.[21] The best edition to work with currently is the four-volume 1979 edition produced by Louis Cooper, but since it privileges *GCU-S*, inconsistently provides rejected readings and also ignores MS 1920, it cannot be considered complete, particularly for the section on the First Crusade, our concern here.[22] Since the manuscripts, particularly MS 1920, present quite different readings, evocative of the *laisses similaires* and epic features of the source material, this article works directly from the manuscripts where they survive.[23]

The array of manuscripts, and *GCU-S*, present quite a contradictory picture of the patronage of the compilation. The 1503 print prologue, not paralleled in any manuscript, attributes patronage to Alfonso X 'the Wise' of Castile (1252–84), as does the Salamanca MS 1698 at another juncture.[24] However, two of the other manuscripts (MS 1920 but also the oldest of the four, MS 1187) instead indicate that his successor, Sancho IV 'the Brave' (1284–95), was behind the assembly of the work.[25] The originality of the *GCU-S* prologue is dubious, furthermore, since it matches very closely that found in the sixteenth-century printings of the *Bocados de oro*.[26] Perhaps composition of the *GCU* began under Alfonso and was completed under Sancho, that is, it was undergoing translation and compilation throughout the 1280s and into the early 1290s.[27] On the basis of a reference in the *Castigos* of Sancho IV, composed between

1293 and 1295, a likely end date for the compilation can be established.[28] Besides, MS 1187 appears to be late thirteenth-century in date, and perhaps constituted part of the original royally commissioned copy.[29] Thus, the *GCU* was almost certainly compiled in the Castilian court in the late thirteenth century, using manuscripts of an array of Old French texts, and perhaps incorporating the work of multiple translators, subsequently compiled into one relatively coherent narrative – although sometimes contradictory versions of the same event find their way into the text.[30]

The most substantial source is the *Eracles* translation of William of Tyre with continuations associated particularly with the Colbert-Fontainebleau redaction.[31] Translations from this text, and not its Latin counterpart, provide the skeleton of the *GCU*, and from after the First Crusade section (Book 3, Chapter 78 in *GCU-S*'s division), the *GCU* is simply a translation of the *Eracles*. Into this framework, passages from various other sources are interwoven. An extensive digression, all under one chapter (Book 2, Chapter 43) in *GCU-S*, but preserved in smaller subdivisions in MS 1920, gives a prosification of the Carolingian-focused *Mainet* and *Berte aux grands pieds*. This material is clumsily linked to the crusade story: the crusader Fulcher Boel of Chartres is introduced as an ancestor of Charlemagne, giving the opportunity for the *GCU* to springboard into this digression on the emperor's youth. The introduction of this material may have taken place after the rest of the compilation was completed; Bautista suggests the second half of the fourteenth century.[32] The digression that was more likely present in the original compilation is that of the Swan Knight material (*Naissance du chevalier au cygne, Chevalier au cygne, Enfances Godefroy*) on Godfrey of Bouillon's ancestors, also taken from the Old French Crusade Cycle.[33] Initially probably interwoven narratively after Godfrey's death, the prominence and placement of this material was probably emended in subsequent drafts of the *GCU*, reflecting growing interest in the Swan Knight material in the court of Sancho IV.[34]

Turning to its sources for the First Crusade, the *GCU* provides quite extensive information. It considers Richard the Pilgrim (mentioned in the *Antioche*) to be identical with the canon of St Peter's in Antioch 'ki le cançon fist' ('who made this song') (referred to in the 'Sathanas' episode of the *Chétifs*, where it is revealed that the committing of this story to writing was patronised by Raymond of Poitiers, 'qi ceste estoire ama', 'who loved this story').[35] Subsequently, in the *GCU*, Richard's name is flagged as a source for material from the extant *Jérusalem*;[36] the

Antioche;³⁷ and the *Chétifs*.³⁸ While it is possible that the *GCU* had information no longer available to us on Richard, more likely the compiler had access to an *OFCC* manuscript which did not include the *Antioche* prologue where Graindor's name is found (such as Paris, Bibliothèque nationale de France, Arsenal MS 3139, London, British Library, MS Add. 36615 and Paris, Bibliothèque nationale de France, MS fr. 12569), combined the two oblique references to authorship in the central trilogy, and induced a 'Richard, pilgrim and canon of Saint-Peter's in Antioch' as the author of the whole. In MS 1920, one of the attributions to Richard (an expansion of that of the *Chétifs*, which the *GCU* is translating at this point) contains detailed additional information on the other sources not used at this particular juncture but evidently serving as sources elsewhere: 'nin del libro de la estoria mayor de ultramar, nin del libro de Gregorio de las Torres, nin del limoji, nin del libro del Grano Dorado de As' ('Not in the Book of the Great History of Outremer, nor in the Book of Gregory of Lastours, nor in [the Book] of Limoges, nor in the Book of Graindor of Douai').³⁹ The clear enthusiasm for distinguishing between these texts implies that the compilation used five First Crusade sources:

1. The *Estoria mayor de Ultramar*, understood as the *Eracles*.
2. The 'Book of Richard the Pilgrim', composed at the behest of Prince Raymond of Antioch.
3. The 'Book of Graindor of Douai'.
4. The 'Book of Gregory (Bechada) of Lastours'.
5. The 'Book of Limoges'.

One of [2] or [3] was clearly the extant *OFCC* central trilogy; while one of [4] or [5] almost certainly refers to the extant *Antioca*. The simplest way of resolving the remaining references is to introduce a hypothetical variant-(proto?)-*Antioche* and a variant-(proto?)-*Antioca*; or there may have been other works which served as source material but were separate from these teleologically constructed traditions. But the subdivision of material in the *GCU* not found in our extant texts – *Eracles*/*OFCC*/*Antioca* fragment – based on its likely source remains a thorny problem.

Attempts to delineate what material comes from which hypothetical or lost text has thus far involved determining which crusaders are discussed most intensely and positively in any given passage, and then ascribing this passage to a putative regionally focused work. Gaston Paris was the first to pioneer this approach, identifying sections of the *GCU* which were fixated on the heroics of southern French crusaders, and suggesting that they had been part of the *Chanson d'Antioche provençale* (the *Antioca*) of which the Madrid fragment was the surviving part.[40] His approach was adopted wholesale by Northup, who created a table of sources pinpointing which hypothetical source was putatively being used (subsequently serving as the base for a similar table by Cooper).[41] Christine Rumpf Stresau, in 1977, went further and hypothesised a lost epic source called 'Boymonte', serving as the source for the unattributable material highlighting Italo-Norman crusaders.[42] More cautiously, admitting that 'information on Occitan participants ... is reasonably assigned to the Occitan tradition' but stopping short of saying it derived from a proto-*Antioca*, Carol Sweetenham and Linda Paterson followed along similar lines, providing a delineation of scenes which the *GCU* implies were in the full *Antioca*.[43] Any passages which have no obvious affiliation to a group of crusaders can be placed in the hold-all category 'unidentified lost source'.

The flaws of such an approach are patent. First, it implies that tightly focused regional texts on the First Crusade existed at one point, recounting only the activities of knights from a particular area; whilst in fact all of the epic texts that we have access to demonstrate extensive ranges of interest and combine the deeds of knights from a wide geographical area. These narratives display a high degree of interrelation. The Occitan *Antioca* fragment ascribes a dominant role to, and glowing praise for, Count Robert of Flanders.[44] Fulcher Boel of Chartres, not a major lord and a likely candidate for being a feature of a regional tradition, is also prominently featured in the *Antioca*.[45] Wicher the Swabian appears very frequently in the northern French *Antioche*.[46] Gouffier of Lastour's heroism was recorded in the *Eracles*, whence it found its way into the *GCU*.[47] By defining a subjectively selected assortment of unattributable material relating to the actions of heroes from the Languedoc, say, and calling this the proto-*Antioca*, the very concept of regional text creation is reinforced and perpetuated without any evidence that this delineation is even conceptually valid. The fictive constructed text can then become an agent for 'influence' on any extant text which mentions these heroes. The end result of such an approach would be a categorisation of the mass of epic narration found in the vernacular First Crusade texts into individual compartmentalised 'original sources' linked to seigneurial houses. This is not to say that such rationales are necessarily wrong, or indeed intellectually unproductive. Such a method may unveil the outline of a proto-*Antioche* or proto-*Antioca*, but 'unveiling' here veers uncomfortably close to 'inventing'. Certainty would be much more obtainable if future analyses of the *GCU*'s sources are carried out with an eye on linguistic, orthographical and stylistic influences in combination with identifying the characters in focus.

Ranged against this note of caution is the unavoidable truth that the status of certain families in these texts strongly suggests an influence of patronage, support or local patterns of memorialisation. That most discussed is the influence of the lords of Saint-Pol visible in the extant *Antioche*, most notably highlighted by Duparc-Quioc in 1970 and Sweetenham in 2006.[48] Together, 'Count' Hugh (?–1130) and his son Enguerrand of Saint-Pol (?–1099) are mentioned well over sixty times, putting them among the front rank of heroes. Influenced by her assessment of Graindor as merely a late reviser, Duparc-Quioc situated the involvement of the Saint-Pols around Richard the Pilgrim's original *Antioche*, a text which she claimed would have influenced the prominent role afforded to the two in Albert of Aachen's *Historia*.[49] Sweetenham, on the other hand, linked the Saint-Pols' prominence in the *Antioche* to the involvement of this family in the Third and Fourth Crusades, when they became both prominent crusade leaders and patrons of vernacular literature (including sponsoring the Old French translation of the *Pseudo-Turpin*).[50] This, she argued, provided a fitting context for the introduction of the deeds of the Saint-Pols into the *Antioche* tradition, when the family had most to gain from emphasising their prior crusade involvement. It is conversely also true, however, that a family tradition of meritorious crusading activity, harking back to the First Crusade, embodied in the patronage of songs, could have provided inspiration to the members of the family who joined Philip Augustus and subsequently the 1202–4 expedition. The Saint-Pols had been among the most important and powerful vassals of Theobald of Flanders, a lord who clearly saw the value in departing for the East. Political advantages in portraying one's family's involvement in the 1096–9 expedition might well have been substantial from the mid-twelfth century.[51] Sweetenham's general concept was expanded in Edgington and Sweetenham's 2011 translation, a hypothesised 'Saint-Pol text' (c. 1200) now being proposed, subsequently incorporated into the cyclical *remaniement* of the *Antioche*.[52] The idea that an important noble family might provide support, financial or otherwise, to an epic poet composing a song on Antioch is supported by the famous passage of Lambert of Ardres, where Arnold of Ardres, despite being a distinguished First Crusader, was omitted from the crusade *chanson* for having refused a *scurra* (an epic poet) a pair of scarlet slippers.[53] But patronage such as this is just as likely to support oral, sung narratives, as in Lambert's example, as written ones. I suggest that the *GCU* constitutes part of a body of evidence (most notably alongside the 'G manuscript' of Baldric of Bourgueil's *Historia*) which demonstrates that neither is the Saint-Pol influence restricted to the surviving textual manifestation of the *Antioche*, nor was the creation of a 'Saint-Pol text' precursor (oral or written) likely to have taken place in such temporal proximity to the composition of the extant *Antioche*.

The *GCU* consistently presents the Saint-Pols as heroes of the crusade story, even when not translating the extant *Antioche*. Along with Rotrou of Perche, Gouffier of Lastours, and many knights from the south of France, Enguerrand is involved in a desperate assault on Soliman's forces at Dorylaeum.[54] During a battle over the Orontes, Enguerrand, riding a horse transfixed with arrows, finds a ford by which the river may be crossed, and informs his fellow knights, causing a bloody rout among the enemy Turks.[55] Immediately after this, the elder Saint-Pol, Hugh, addresses the other Christian leaders, reminding them of their holy mission and urging them to set up an ambush.[56] Hugh fights a formulaic combat outside Antioch against a pagan emir called Foruc, absorbing a lance blow on his hauberk before transfixing the Saracen and throwing him dead to the ground.[57] The most extensive passage on the Saint-Pols uniquely in the *GCU* concerns a council of nobles outside Antioch. This comes to a head when Hugh interrupts, to say, in a lengthy prayer, that no matter if the report of advancing enemies is true, the Christians have God's protection and will triumph. The *GCU* then devotes a full column to the 'white-haired' count's virtues: generous to his knights, hospitable to the poor, and without motive, except love of God, for being on crusade.[58] None of these are paralleled directly in the extant *Antioche*.

Similarly, the 'G' manuscript of Baldric's *Historia* – a twelfth-century manuscript, probably produced in the Touraine around the middle of that century – also contains epic themed material on the Saint-Pols, which seemingly derives from a source shared by the *GCU* and the *Antioche*.[59] In one episode, Enguerrand and Hugh of Saint-Pol, father and son, fight side by side at Antioch competing in hurling over their enemies with Ralph of Beaugency, until the elder, Count Hugh, teases his son: 'Vetulus bos praevalet iuniori!'[60] An identical taunt is found in the *Antioche*, but transferred to take place at Nicaea (still with Ralph):

'Mius valt vace que veel!' ('The old bull is worth more than the calf!').[61] But to find the second half of this anecdote, and the payoff of the joke, we must turn to the *GCU*. Here, at Antioch, Enguerrand rescues Hugh from death at the hands of a pagan, taunting in return: 'Mas vale un buen novillo para tirar la carreta que un par de bueyes viejos!' ('But a bullock is worth more in pulling a cart than a pair of old oxen!').[62] The full exchange is not complete in any one account, so it is reasonable to assume all to be drawing on a narrative (oral or written), which highlighted the Saint-Pols' deeds, extant by around the mid-twelfth century. Nor is this the only colourful anecdote about the Saint-Pols uniquely in 'G': when the crusaders are riding out to fight the pagans at the great battle of Antioch, Enguerrand jokes with the bishop of Orange, who is blessing the troops with water, not to be so liberal in his splashing.[63]

Both *GCU* and 'G' present evidence, therefore, that the Saint-Pol influence is not to be located solely in the extant *Antioche*, but is a more widely distributed, and older, feature of First Crusade narrative. The 'Saint-Pol text' could still have existed, but if so, it predated the production of 'G', and thus would have been exerting an influence by, at the latest, *c.* 1175. Alternatively, these echoes of the foregrounding of the Saint-Pols might have been a feature of an early proto-*Antioche* (oral or written) divergent from the current redaction of the *Antioche* but which influenced the creation of 'G' and was transmitted into the *GCU* – we have seen that the compilation ostensibly used two versions ('Richard's' and 'Graindor's'). It is worth noting that the Saint-Pols were long-standing patrons, from 1141 at the latest, of the abbey of Fécamp, which plays a prominent role in the *Chétifs* – its abbot is even (ahistorically) one of the captives.[64] There is no way of knowing if the *Antioca*, or Bechada, also emphasised the deeds of the Saint-Pols, although they are often found among contingents of southern knights in the *GCU*.

So, the *GCU* was drawing on at least one text or orally performed tradition which also influenced the creation of 'G'. The same relationship is observable between the *GCU* and the Anglo-Norman *Siège d'Antioche*; neither is close enough to suggest that one was utilising the other directly, but they clearly share a common ancestor. Since the sources of the *Siège* are quite obscure, this is of foremost interest, although its statement that it was based on the work of 'uns clers provençal' is evocative of a link with the work of the Provençal Bechada.[65]

A set-piece at the Bridge Battle where a crusader swims across the river outside Antioch to hack apart some Turks clinging on to the bridge supports is found, with different figures substituted in, in several First Crusade texts.⁶⁶ In the 'G manuscript' it is Wicher the Swabian; in the *Antioche*, it is Raimbald Craton.⁶⁷ But both the *Siège* and the *GCU* associate this story with Rotrou of Perche and his vassals, although with varying details. In the *Siège*, it is Rotrou's knight, Yves Paen, who is so infuriated by the sight of the pagans on the other side of the river that he crosses the river to attack, before attempting to swim back, wounded, only to be helped by another of Rotrou's knights, Herdoïn, to shore – Rotrou all the while looking on in a tearful panic. Both knights, wounded and experiencing holy visions, subsequently die of exposure. In the *GCU*, it is Rotrou and one of his knights (he had earlier had two, just as in the *Siège*), Yugo, who find themselves trapped while slaughtering the pagans, and swim back across the river, surviving after resting themselves and their horses.⁶⁸ That this story should be associated with Rotrou and his (two) knights in both narratives suggests some degree of shared source material. In the *GCU*, Yugo is Rotrou's cousin. In the *Siège*, Yves is the foster-brother of Herdoïn. As is clear from the example of Hugh/Yugo/Eves of Saint-Pol (n. 58, above), 'Yves' and 'Yugo', the *GCU*'s normal form of 'Hugh', could be easily confused. A text which exalted Rotrou of Perche's activities might seem a likely candidate for a *langue d'oïl* regional tradition, but Rotrou had connections with several of the figures which seem to be foregrounded in the extant *Antioca* (and presumably the earlier work of Bechada). Rotrou of Perche would, subsequently to the crusade, serve with Gaston of Béarn and other southern lords in Spain.⁶⁹ His sister Mathilda married first Raymond of Turenne, and then subsequently Guy of Lastours, nephew of Gouffier.⁷⁰ Intriguingly, the story of Rotrou's swim in the *GCU* is integrated into one of William of Montpellier and Gaston of Béarn protecting the barbican of a fortification against attack.

A further example also suggests the *Siège* and the *GCU* shared source material. When the crusaders decide to send to the emperor Alexios requesting a navy to blockade Nicaea (a request which does not feature in the *Antioche*), only the *GCU* and the *Siège* depict the message being carried by two knights, travelling alone. In the *Siège*, these are 'Symons qui de France fud nez / et li autre Reignier, mult preuz et mult senez' ('Simon, who was born in France (presumably Île-de-France) / and the other, Reignier, a very old and very valiant man'), whereas in the *GCU* they are 'Rruberte de Sordas et el otro Beltran de Lis' ('Robert of Sordas and the other, Beltran de Lis').⁷¹ None of these figures can be identified with certainty (although the first in the *GCU* may be Robert of Sourdeval). What follows in both texts confirms the interrelation between them. The two crusader companions are described arriving in Constantinople, asking for the whereabouts of the emperor, and finding him in a garden or meadow, *huerta* in the Spanish, *prez* in the Old French, before recounting their demands for galleys and another kind of ship (*etnekes et galies* in the Old French, *galeas e otros navios* in the Spanish) to the emperor. No other First Crusade text describes this meeting in such detail; the most convincing hypothesis is that the two accounts were drawing on a shared source.

The material regarding Hugh, Enguerrand, and Rotrou in the *GCU* demonstrates that the heroic emphases of vernacular crusade accounts cannot be neatly compartmentalised into a framework of influences exerted by regional texts linked to early thirteenth-century patronage. By the time written evidence of the crusade vernacular epic emerges in the late twelfth century, it seems as if several narrative traditions had already become interwoven. To extricate them is deeply challenging. However, if any elucidation of the development of epic First Crusade narrative before the date of the earliest manuscripts of the *OFCC* is possible, it will have to proceed from a full analysis of the content and style of the *GCU*.

Notes

1. GCU-S is *La gran conquista de Ultramar*, ed. H. Giesser (Salamanca, 1503).
2. With the exception of the sections preserving Swan Knight material, edited separately: *La leyenda del Caballero del Çisne*, ed. E. Mazorriaga (Madrid, 1914); C. B. Fitch, 'El Cavallero del Cisne: a critical edition' (unpublished PhD dissertation, University of Kentucky, 1974).
3. G. T. Northup, 'La *Gran conquista de Ultramar* and its Problems', *Hispanic Review*, 2 (1934), 287–302 (here 296).
4. The first major contributions being *La Chanson d'Antioche, composée au commencement du XIIe siecle par le Pélerin Richard, renouvelée sous le règne de Philippe Auguste par Graindor de Douai*, ed. P. Paris, 2 vols (Paris, 1848); *Le Chevalier au cygne et Godefroid de Bouillon*, ed. F. A. F. T. de Reiffenberg (Brussels, 1846). The other major text which remains unedited in full is the *Siège d'Antioche* (discussed below).
5. *OFCC*, vol. 4 (*La Chanson d'Antioche*, ed. J. A. Nelson (2003)); *ChAnt*; *The Chanson d'Antioche: An Old French Account of the First Crusade*, trans. S. B. Edgington and C. Sweetenham (Farnham, 2011).
6. 'He who made the song ... Richard the Pilgrim'; *OFCC*, vol. 4, pp. 49, 337; *ChAnt*, vol. 1, pp. 19, 443. The exact meaning of 'faire + cançon' is hard to pin down: it could be to compose, to sing, to craft the general structure, or even to commit to writing.
7. See R. F. Cook, *'Chanson d'Antioche': Chanson de geste, le Cycle de la croisade est-il épique?* (Amsterdam, 1980); H. Kleber, 'Wer ist der Verfasser der Chanson d'Antioche? Revision

einer Streitfrage', *Zeitschrift für französische Sprache und Literatur*, 94 (1984), 115–42; H. Kleber, 'Graindor de Douai: Remanieur-Auteur-Mécène?', in K. H. Bender (ed.), *Les Épopées de la croisade: Premier colloque international (Trèves, 6–11 Août 1984), Zeitschrift für Französische Sprache und Literatur* (Stuttgart, 1987), pp. 66–75; *Chanson d'Antioche*, trans. Edgington and Sweetenham, pp. 3–8.

8   *ChAnt*, vol. 2, pp. 143–242; *Chanson d'Antioche*, trans. Edgington and Sweetenham, *passim*, but pp. 60–1. For an excellent synthesis, S. B. Edgington, 'Romance and Reality in the Sources for the Sieges of Antioch, 1097–1098', in C. Dendrinos *et al.* (eds), *Porphyrogenita: Essays on the History and Literature of Byzantium and the Latin East in Honour of Julian Chrysostomides* (Aldershot, 2003), pp. 33–47.

9   Duparc-Quioc considered that the *GCU* proved this: S. Duparc-Quioc, 'La Chanson de Jérusalem et la Gran Conquista de Ultramar', *Romania*, 66 (1940), 32–48. But see Cook, 'Chanson d'Antioche', p. 10; N. R. Thorp, 'La *Gran Conquista de Ultramar* et les origines de la *Chanson de Jérusalem*', in Bender (ed.), *Épopées*, pp. 76–83.

10 *The Chanson des Chétifs and Chanson de Jérusalem: Completing the Central Trilogy of the Old French Crusade Cycle*, trans. C. Sweetenham (Farnham, 2016), pp. 7–21.

11 *Chanson de la croisade albigeoise*, ed. E. Martin-Chabot, 3 vols (Paris, 1931–61), vol. 3, pp. xv, 8. For a highly questionable reconstruction of the song of Bechada and its subsequent influence, based mainly in Gaston Paris's work on the *GCU*, see J.-F. Gareyte, *L'Aube des Troubadours: La Chanson d'Antioche du chevalier Béchade* (Périgueux, 2007).

12 Geoffrey of Vigeois, 'Chronica Gaufredi coenobitae monasterii D. Martialis Lemovicensis, ac prioris Vosiensis coenobii', in *Novae bibliothecae manuscript[orum] librorum*, ed. P. Labbé, 2 vols (Paris, 1657), vol. 2, pp. 279–342 (here p. 296).

13 S. T. Parsons, 'A Unique Song of the First Crusade? New Observations on the Hatton 77 Manuscript of the *Siège d'Antioche*', in L. M. Paterson and S. T. Parsons (eds), *Literature of the Crusades* (Woodbridge, 2018), pp. 55–74.

14 N. L. Paul, *To Follow in their Footsteps: The Crusades and Family Memory in the High Middle Ages* (Ithaca, NY, 2012), pp. 174–6.

15 F. Bautista, 'La composición de la *Gran conquista de Ultramar*', *Revista de Literatura Medieval*, 17 (2005), 33–70 (here 37–8); C. González, *La tercera crónica de Alfonso X: 'La gran conquista de Ultramar'* (London, 1992), pp. 127–8. All the BNE manuscripts are consultable at: <http://www.bne.es/es/Catalogos/BibliotecaDigitalHispanica/Inicio/index.html> (last accessed 3 January 2019).

16 C. González, 'Gran Conquista de Ultramar, La', in E. M. Gerli (ed.), *Medieval Iberia: An Encyclopedia* (London, 2003), pp. 367–8 (here p. 367).

17 In addition to the partial editions referred to in n. 2, there is also an edition of the section dealing with Saladin's conquests: *Old Spanish Grammar of 'La gran conquista de Ultramar', with Critical Edition of Book IV, Chapters 126–193: The Conquest of Jerusalem by Sultan Saladin*, ed. V. Honsa (New York, 1986), as well as three unpublished dissertations by J. R. Whipple, '"La gran conquista de ultramar", Book IV, Chapters 1–57, critical edition, a study of the Old French sources, grammatical analysis and glossary' (unpublished PhD dissertation, University of Michigan (Ann Arbor, 1973)), H. N. Bershas, 'A critical edition of "La gran conquista de ultramar", Book IV, Chapters 194–288' (unpublished PhD dissertation, University of Michigan (Ann Arbor, 1946)) and G. Stanley Calbick, 'A critical text of "La gran conquista de ultramar", Chapters CCLXIV–CCC' (unpublished PhD dissertation, University of Chicago, 1939), all editing sections from Book Four, well after the First Crusade narrative.

18 *La gran conquista de Ultramar*, ed. P. de Gayangos (Madrid, 1858).

19. Distributed to libraries under the titles: 'Text and Concordance of the *Gran conquista de Ultramar*: BNM R-518, R-519', ed. R. Harris-Northall (Madison, WI, 1994); and 'Text and Concordances of Biblioteca Nacional Manuscript 1187: *Gran conquista de Ultramar*', ed. F. M. Waltman and L. Cooper (Madison, WI, 1985).
20. *La gran conquista de Ultramar: Biblioteca Nacional MS 1187*, ed. L. Cooper and F. M. Waltman (Madison, WI, 1989).
21. *La leyenda del Caballero del Cisne*, ed. M. T. Echenique (Barcelona, 1989).
22. *La gran conquista de Ultramar*, ed. L. Cooper, 4 vols (Bogotá, 1979) (hereafter *GCU*-Cooper).
23. See Bautista, 'La composición de la *Gran conquista de Ultramar*', 43–5.
24. *GCU*-Cooper, vol. 1, p. 2; *GCU*, ed. Gayangos, p. xii. Gayangos attributes this passage, however, to the wrong Alfonso; see C. González, 'Alfonso X el Sabio y *La gran conquista de Ultramar*', *Hispanic Review*, 54 (1986), 67–82 (here 70–1).
25. *La gran conquista de Ultramar: Biblioteca Nacional MS 1187*, ed. Cooper and Waltman, p. 258. MS 1187, fol. 360v; MS 1920, fol. 204v. MS 1187 misnumbers Alfonso as the eleventh of his name, and Sancho as the sixth, rather than tenth and fourth respectively.
26. *GCU*, ed. Gayangos, pp. v–vi, 1.
27. González, 'Alfonso X el Sabio'.
28. C. Dominguez Prieto, 'La *Grant estoria de Ultramar* (conocida como *Gran conquista de Ultramar*) de Sancho IV y la *Estoire de Eracles empereur et la conqueste de la terre d'Outremer*', *Incipit*, 25–6 (2005–6), 189–212 (here 201, n. 14). Bautista, 'La composición de la *Gran conquista de Ultramar*', 34.
29. C. Dominguez Prieto, 'Gran conquista de Ultramar', in G. Dunphy *et al.* (eds), *Encyclopedia of the Medieval Chronicle*, 2 vols (Leiden, 2010), vol. 1, pp. 726–7.
30. There is still debate, however, over whether the compilation was carried out in France, and subsequently translated in Spain, as most recently suggested in J. M. Q. Sanz, *Cruzadas y literatura: El Caballero del Cisne y la legenda genealógica de Godofredo de Bouillon* (Madrid, 2000), p. 63. But see Dominguez Prieto, '*Grant estoria*', 192–4. For variant opinions on the success of the *GCU*'s attempts to interweave different versions of the same story, see *ChAnt*, vol. 1, p. 306; C. Dominguez Prieto, 'Antiocha la noble fue ganada assí como avéys oýdo: Traducción y *double emploi* en la *Gran conquista de Ultramar* (II, 73)', in J. Paredes and E. M. Raya (eds), *Traducir la Edad Media: La traducción de la literatura medieval románica* (Granada, 1999), pp. 349–61 (here pp. 359–61).
31. The manuscript used must have been of a similar type to Paris, Bibliothèque nationale de France, MS fr. 2628. See Domínguez, '*Grant estoria*', 202–8. This manuscript also contains revealingly similar mistakes, then translated into Castilian. See the incorrect separation of Walter Sansavoir's name as 'Gautier sanz saver' in MS fr. 2628, fol. 9r, <https://gallica.bnf.fr/ark:/12148/btv1b9058864v/f10.item> (last accessed 3 January 2019). This is subsequently translated into Spanish as 'Galter sin saber' ('Ignorant Walter'); see Northup, 'La *Gran conquista de Ultramar* and its Problems', 289.
32. F. Bautista, 'Sobre la materia carolingia en la *Gran conquista de Ultramar* y en la *Crónica fragmentaria*', *Hispanic Research Journal*, 3/3 (2002), 209–26 (here 223).
33. The version of *Naissance* is different from any extant: W. R. J. Barron, 'Versions and Texts of the *Naissance du chevalier au cygne*', *Romania*, 356 (1968), 481–538 (here 483 n. 1).
34. Bautista, 'Composición', 49–51. Sancho's accounts for 1294 indicate the purchase of a sumptuous 'Throne of the Swan Knight', F. Guttiérez-Baños, *Las empresas artísticas de Sancho IV el Bravo* (Valladolid, 1997), p. 226; Bautista, 'Composición', 47–51, and letters from James II of Aragon *c.* 1314 mention a book which prominently features the Swan Knight story, 'que fue del rey de Castiella, de las istorias de la conquista de Antiocha e de

istorias de los signos [viz. *cisnes*]' ('Which belonged to the king of Castille, of the histories of the conquest of Antioch and of the histories of the swans'), perhaps the *GCU* or one of the *OFCC*: *Castigos e documentos para bien vivir ordenados por el rey Don Sancho IV*, ed. A. Rey (Bloomington, 1952), p. 20.

35   *The Chanson des Chétifs and Chanson de Jérusalem*, trans. Sweetenham, pp. 9–16.
36   *GCU*-Cooper, vol. 2, p. 520.
37   MS 1920, fol. 150v; *GCU*-Cooper, vol. 2, pp. 225–6.
38   MS 1920, fols 203v and 204v.
39   MS 1920, fol. 204v. For the *OFCC* manuscript used by the *GCU* compiler, see Kleber, 'Verfasser', 127.
40   G. Paris, 'La *Chanson d'Antioche* provençale et la *Gran conquista de Ultramar*', *Romania*, 17 (1888), 513–41; 19 (1890), 562–91; 22 (1893), 345–63 (1888–93).
41   Northup, 'La *Gran conquista de Ultramar* and its Problems', 296–302; for his approach, see 292; *GCU*-Cooper, vol. 4, pp. 326–40.
42   C. Rumpf Stresau, '*La gran conquista de Ultramar*: its Sources and Composition' (unpublished PhD dissertation, University of North Carolina at Chapel Hill, 1977), 2, 169–84.
43   *The Canso d'Antioca: An Occitan Epic Chronicle of the First Crusade*, ed. and trans. C. Sweetenham and L. M. Paterson (Aldershot, 2003), pp. 33–43. See also Bautista, 'Composición', 35–6.
44   *Canso d'Antioca*, ed. and trans. Sweetenham and Paterson, pp. 221–3; *ChAnt*, vol. 2, p. 180.
45   *Canso d'Antioca*, ed. and trans. Sweetenham and Paterson, pp. 202, 230, 236.
46   *ChAnt*, vol. 1, p. 558.
47   A point made in *Canso d'Antioca*, ed. and trans. Sweetenham and Paterson, p. 30.
48   S. Duparc-Quioc, 'Recherches sur l'origine des poèmes épiques de croisade et leur utilisation éventuelle par les grandes familles féodales', in *Problemi attuali di scienza e di cultura: Atti del convegno internazionale sul tema: La poesia epica e la sua formazione* (Roma, 28 marzo–3 aprile 1969) (Rome, 1970), pp. 771–92 (and also discussed in *ChAnt*, vol. 2, pp. 231–4); C. Sweetenham, 'Antioch and Flanders: Some Reflections on the Writing of the *Chanson d'Antioche*', in P. E. Bennett, A. E. Cobby and J. E. Everson (eds), *Epic and Crusade: Proceedings of the Société Rencesvals British Branch held at Lucy Cavendish College, Cambridge, 27–28 March 2004* (Edinburgh, 2006), pp. 131–51.
49   Duparc-Quioc, 'Recherches', pp. 773–4, 784. See also AA, pp. 212–17; S. B. Edgington, 'Albert of Aachen and the *Chansons de geste*', in J. France and W. G. Zajac (eds), *The Crusades and their Sources: Essays Presented to Bernard Hamilton* (Aldershot, 1998), pp. 23–37 .
50   G. M. Spiegel, *Romancing the Past: The Rise of Vernacular Prose Historiography in Thirteenth-Century France* (Berkeley, CA, 1993), p. 70.
51   For the power of the Saint-Pol family in Picardy during the twelfth century, see R. Fossier, *La Terre et les Hommes en Picardie jusqu'à la fin du XIIIe siècle*, 2 vols (Paris, 1968), vol. 2, pp. 658, 682, 686. For their later crusading involvement, see pp. 610–11, particularly n. 91; H. J. Tanner, *Families, Friends, and Allies: Boulogne and Politics in Northern France and England, c. 879–1160* (Leiden, 2003), p. 224.
52   *Chanson d'Antioche*, trans. Edgington and Sweetenham, pp. 20–4.
53   Lambert of Ardres, *Chronique de Guines et d'Ardre*, ed. Marquis de Godefroy-Menilglaise (Paris, 1855), p. 311; Lambert of Ardres, *The History of the Counts of Guines and Lords of Ardres*, trans. L. Shopkow (Philadelphia, 2001), pp. 164–5.
54   *GCU*-Cooper, vol. 1, p. 452.
55   *GCU*-Cooper, vol. 1, p. 497. Although Enguerrand does find a path across the Orontes in the *Antioche*, the specifics are entirely different and it seems as if the two passages have come from separate sources.

56 *GCU*-Cooper, vol. 1, pp. 499–500.
57 *GCU*-Cooper, vol. 2, p. 19; MS 1920, fol. 65r.
58 On the unusual nature of this passage, see Rumpf Stresau, '*La gran conquista de Ultramar*: Its Sources and Composition', 172–5. Hugh is here referred to as *Eves*: 'esto conde de San Polo era padre de don Jaran e avia nombre Eves' ('This count of Saint-Pol was the father of Lord Enguerrand and had the name Eves'), MS 1920, fols 46v–47r, *GCU*-Cooper, vol. 1, p. 604, although elsewhere he is referred to as *Yugo*. Cf. *GCU*-Cooper, vol. 1, p. 501; MS 1920, fol. 65r. Probably the Old French oblique case of Hugh, 'Huon', has been misread as the Old French oblique case of Yves, 'Yvon'.
59 N. Paul, 'Crusade, Memory, and Regional Politics in Twelfth-Century Amboise', *Journal of Medieval History*, 31/2 (2005), 127–41 (esp. 139–40).
60 BB, p. 46, n. f.
61 *ChAnt*, vol. 1, p. 83; *OFCC*, vol. 4, p. 97
62 *GCU*-Cooper, vol. 1, p. 533. On this, see *La Chanson d'Antioche*, ed. Paris, vol. 1, p. 537, n. 1; S. Duparc-Quioc, 'La Composition de la *Chanson d'Antioche*', *Romania*, 83 (1962), 1–29, 210–47 (here 242–3). The taunt is present in MS 1920, fol. 10v, but here reads 'mas val un mancebo en la batalla que un par de viejos!' ('A young man is worth more in the fight than a pair of old ones!').
63 Not recorded in Biddlecombe's edition, BB, p. 79. See instead Baldric of Bourgueil, 'Historia Jerosolimitana', in *Recueil des historiens des croisades: Historiens occidentaux* (hereafter *RHC. Occ.*), 5 vols (Paris, 1844–95), vol. 4, pp. 1–112 (here p. 76, n. 1). Or the manuscript at <https://gallica.bnf.fr/ark:/12148/btv1b9078409t/f40> (last accessed 3 January 2019). This scene is paralleled in the extant *Antioche*: *ChAnt*, vol. 1, p. 402; *OFCC*, vol. 4, p. 313.
64 *Les chartes des comtes de Saint-Pol (XIe–XIIIe siècles)*, ed. J.-F. Nieus (Turnhout, 2008), pp. 90, 184; G. M. Myers, 'Le développement des *Chétifs*: La version Fécampoise?', in Bender (ed.), *Épopées*, pp. 84–90; *The Chanson des Chétifs and Chanson de Jérusalem*, trans. Sweetenham, p. 19.
65 *La Chanson de la Première Croisade en ancien français d'après Baudri de Bourgueil: Édition et analyse lexicale*, ed. J. Gabel de Aguirre (Heidelberg, 2015), p. 115.
66 C. Sweetenham, 'What Really Happened to Eurvin de Créel's Donkey? Anecdotes in Sources for the First Crusade', in M. Bull and D. Kempf (eds), *Writing the Early Crusades: Text, Transmission and Memory* (Woodbridge, 2014), pp. 75–88 (pp. 80, 82).
67 Not recorded in Biddlecombe's edition, BB, p. 51. See instead *RHC Occ.*, vol. 4, p. 50, n. 15, or the manuscript at https://gallica.bnf.fr/ark:/12148/btv1b9078409t/f23 (last accessed 3 January 2019); *ChAnt*, vol. 1, pp. 208–11; *OFCC*, vol. 4, pp. 174–7.
68 MS 1920, fols 111v and 112r; *GCU*-Cooper, vol. 2, p. 125. For Yves Paen in the *Siège d'Antioche*, see R. Grillo, 'Encore la Perche et la Première Croisade: Remarques sur un "épisode percheron" dans la version française de l'*Historia jerosolimitana* de Baudri de Bourgueil', *Cahiers percherons*, 99/4 (1999), 1–18.
69 L. H. Nelson, 'Rotrou of Perche and the Aragonese Reconquest', *Traditio*, 26 (1970), 113–33; K. Thompson, 'Family Tradition and the Crusading Impulse: The Rotrou Counts of the Perche', *Medieval Prosopography*, 19 (1998), 1–33.
70 'Chronicon Lemovicense', in *Recueil des historiens des Gaules et de la France*, 24 vols (Paris, 1738–1904), vol. 12, p. 424.
71 *Chanson de la Première Croisade*, ed. Gabel de Aguirre, p. 193; MS 2454, fol. 213r; *GCU*-Cooper, vol. 1, p. 418.

INDEX

A
Acre, city of 42, 46
Adela of Blois 38
Adhémar of Le Puy 21, 38, 44, 58–60
Aird, William 38
al-Aqsa mosque 45
Albert of Aachen 6–7, 10, 12, 44, 54–6, 58, 108
Alexios I Komnenos 9, 111
Alfonso X 'The Wise', king of Castile 104
Allen Smith, Katherine 10
Amalric, king of Jerusalem 51, 56
Anglo-Norman 9, 102, 103, 110
Antioch,
    city of 1, 105–6
    sieges of 1–12, 18, 23–4, 26, 27–8, 29, 38, 39, 56–9, 93, 109, 110
    battle of 1–12, 24, 45, 57, 58, 60–1, 84, 88, 90, 93, 110–11
Arnold II 'The Old' of Ardres 108–9

B
Baldric of Bourgeuil 5, 8, 9, 25–6, 41, 54, 57, 58
    G manuscript of his *Historia* 109
Baldwin of Boulogne,
    crusader 4, 42, 53, 87, 89
    count of Edessa 42–4
    king of Jerusalem 35, 42–4, 46
Baldwin III, king of Jerusalem 58
Baldwin IV, king of Jerusalem 51, 56–7
Beirut, city of 43
Beltran de Lis 111
Berte aux grands pieds 105
Bishop of Orange 91, 110
Bocados de oro 104
Bohemond of Taranto, prince of
    Antioch 2, 3, 4, 5, 6, 18, 37, 84

Boymonte, hypothetical epic 107
Brindisi 56

C
Canso d'Antioca 103
Cassidy-Welch, Megan 11–12, 71
Castigos 104–5
Castile 104
Chanson d'Antioche 10, 83–96, 101–3, 105–11
Chanson de la croisade albigeois 103
Chanson des Chétifs 84, 86, 101–3, 105–6, 110
chansons des geste 83–93, 96
Chanson de Jérusalem 84–96, 101–3, 105
Charlemagne 85, 86, 101, 105
Chevalier au cygnet 105
Christ 3, 5, 6, 7, 11, 12, 37, 41, 55–6, 58
    passion of 58, 67–77
Clermont, council of 37, 40, 55
Colbert-Fontainebleau Eracles 105
Conon of Brittany 10
Constantinople, city of 38, 112
Crusade cycle ('cycle rudimentaire') 84–5, 88, 90, 92, 101, 102, 105
Crusades
    1095–9, First 1–12, 17–29, 35–42, 45–6, 51–61, 68–9, 72, 83–96, 101–12
    1101 9, 39
    1189–93, Third 69, 108
    1198–1204, Fourth 72, 108
    1209–29, Albigensian 72, 73–4
    1217–21, Fifth 72
Cubitt, Geoffrey 11–12

D
Dorylaeum, battle of 44, 45, 58, 109

Index

E
Edessa, city of 4, 42, 43–4
Enfances Godefroy 105
Enguerrand of Saint-Pol 108–10, 112
Eracles 101, 105–7
Eustace of Boulogne 53, 87, 89

F
Fécamp, abbey of 110
Fenton, Kirsten 35, 45
Foruc, pagan emir 109
Fulcher Boel of Chartres 105, 107
Fulcher of Chartres 4–5, 6, 7, 8, 9, 24, 36, 38, 39, 42–6, 54, 56, 58–9

G
Gaston of Béarn 111
Geoffrey of Vigeois 103
Gesta Francorum et aliorum Hierosolimitanorum 3, 4, 5, 6, 8, 9, 12, 28, 38, 39, 45, 54, 57
Gilo of Paris 6, 7, 8, 9, 41
Godfrey of Bouillon, ruler of Jerusalem 17, 18, 19, 27, 28, 37, 43, 45, 53, 83–96, 101, 105
Gouffier of Lastours, crusader 103, 107, 109, 111
Graindor of Douai 102, 106, 108, 110
Gran conquista de Ultramar 101–12
Gregory Bechada 103, 106, 110, 111
Guibert of Nogent 5, 8–9, 25, 41

H
Hattin, battle of 12, 69–72, 74, 78
Henry of Huntingdon 54
Heraclius, emperor 101
Herdoïn 111
Holy Lance 2, 3–4, 19, 26, 58, 59, 90
Hugh of Lusignan 39
Hugh of St Pol 108, 109, 111
Hugh of Vermandois 8, 9, 39

I
Ida of Lorraine 53
Île-de-France 111
Iron Bridge 10

J
James II, king of Aragon 105
Jerusalem,
city of 1, 3, 4, 5, 6, 7, 18, 19, 20, 21, 29, 35, 37, 43, 51, 53, 55, 57, 67–78, 83, 86, 88
Holy Sepulchre 1, 3, 5, 6, 17, 28, 29, 37, 39, 45, 55, 67, 69–72, 77, 93, 94–5
siege of 11, 12, 17, 18, 23, 24, 26–9, 39–40, 45, 57, 59–61, 83–96

K
Kerbogha, *atabeg* of Mosul 1, 2, 3, 4, 8, 9, 45, 57
Kostick, Conor 38

L
Lambert of Ardres 108–9
Languedoc 72, 107
Limoges 103, 106
locus amoenus, garden 112
Lucan 40

M
Madrid Fragment, the 103–4, 107
Mainet 105
Matilda II, queen of England 38, 44
Mathilda of Perche 111

N
Nahr al-Kalb, battle of 43
Naissance du chevalier au cygne 105
Nicaea 18, 22–3, 29, 109–10, 111

O
Occitan 67–78, 101, 103, 107
Old French 83–96, 101–2, 105–6, 108, 112
Orderic Vitalis 9
Orontes, river 22–3, 109, 110–11

P
Paul, Nicholas 11, 12, 69
Peire Cardinal 68, 70–3, 78
Peter Bartholomew 58, 59

Index

Peter the Hermit 55, 56, 60, 88, 95
Peter Tudebode 3, 10
   brother of 10
Philip Augustus, king of France 102
Pseudo-Turpin 108

R

Ramla, town of 43 4, 46
Ralph of Caen 6, 7, 8, 9–10
Raimbald Crato 111
Ralph of Beaugency 109
Raymond of Poitiers, prince of Antioch 103, 105, 106
Raymond of Aguilers 3, 8, 9, 18–20, 24, 26, 29, 41, 54, 58
Raymond IV, count of Toulouse 3, 17–22, 26, 29, 58, 68, 72
Raymond VI, count of Toulouse 72
Raymond of Turenne 111
Reignier 111
Richard the Pilgrim 102, 105–6, 108
Robert Curthose, duke of Normandy 45, 87
Robert, count of Flanders 20, 41, 87, 93, 94, 107
Robert, earl of Gloucester 44
Robert of Sourdeval 111–12
Robert the Monk 4–6, 7, 8, 9, 10, 25, 102
Roger of Salerno, prince of Antioch 58
Rosenwein, Barbara 41
Rotrou, count of Perche 109, 111–12

S

Saints
   Demetrius 57, 93
   Dunstan
      Vita Dunstani 40
   George 57, 93
   Mercurius 57, 93
   Wulfstan
      Vita Wulfstani 40
Saint Evroult, abbey of 9
Saint-Pol Text, hypothesised epic 108–11
Saladin 67

Sancho IV 'The Brave', king of Castile 104–5
Sathanas 105
scurra, epic poet 109
Siège d'Antioche 110–12
Soliman of Nicaea 90
Spain 18, 111
Saint Peter's Church, Antioch 106
Stephen of Blois 2, 8, 9, 38, 39, 88
Stephen of Burgundy 39
Stephen of Valence 6, 59
Swan Knight 53–4, 84, 86–7, 101, 105
Symon 111

T

Tancred of Hauteville, prince of Antioch 8, 42, 92
Tarsus, city of 42, 92
Theobald, count of Flanders 108
Thomson, Rodney 40
Thoros, Armenian ruler of Edessa 42–3
Tell Danith, battle of 58
Third Lateran Council 57
Touraine 109
Troubadours 67–78
True Cross
   relic of 12, 59, 69–70, 71, 73
   devotion to 69–77
Turks 22–3, 35, 37, 44–5, 91, 92, 93, 95, 109, 110–11

U

Urban II, pope 17, 18–19, 21, 22, 27, 37, 40, 55

W

Walter the Chancellor 58
Wicher the Swabian 107, 111
William of Malmesbury,
   Gesta Regum Anglorum 24, 35–46
   Histora Novella 36
William of Montpellier 111
William of Tyre 51–61, 101, 105

Y

Yves Paen 111

ISBN 978-1-78683-504-8
eISBN 978-1-78683-505-5
ISSN (Print)   2057-4517
ISSN (Online) 2057-4525
The Journal of Religious History, Literature and Culture
© University of Wales Press, 2019
Articles and reviews © The Contributors, 2019

Contributors to *The Journal of Religious History, Literature and Culture* should refer enquiries to the journal page at www.uwp.co.uk or e-mail press@press.wales. ac.uk requesting notes for contributors.

Advertising enquiries should be sent to the Sales and Marketing Department at the University of Wales Press, at the address below.

Subscriptions: *The Journal of Religious History, Literature and Culture* is published twice a year in June and November. The annual subscription for institutions is £95 (print only), £85 (online only) or £140 (combined); and for individuals is £25 (print or online only) or £40 (combined). Subscription orders should be sent to University of Wales Press, University Registry, King Edward VII Avenue, Cardiff CF10 3NS. E-mail: press@press.wales.ac.uk.

Open Access information for journals is available on the University of Wales Press website at www.uwp.co.uk.